WITH ALL
THEIR HEART

WITH ALL THEIR HEART

TEACHING

YOUR KIDS

TO LOVE GOD

Christine Yount

ISBN: 0-8024-8497-2

1 3 5 7 9 10 8 6 4 2

Printed in the United States of America

To my loving husband, Mike,
and our children—Grant, Abby, and Reed.
When God said, "Delight yourself in Me and
I will give you the desires of your heart,"
He was talking about you.

Contents

ACKNOWLEDGMENTS

Thank you to . . .

My family—immediate and extended—for your support and prayers.

My children's ministry team at work for your friendship and prayers.

RoseAnne Sather, Carmen Kamrath, Albert Cheng, and Tiffany Wagner for your stories of God's work in your lives.

Elsa Mazon for shepherding this book throughout the entire process. You are a helpful sounding board.

Cheryl Dunlop for your skill and insight.

And my heavenly Father, who has given us the amazing Word of God that never runs dry. Thank You for opening up Your Scriptures to help me see truths I have never seen before. I said yes, and You proved once again that You will never disappoint me.

INTRODUCTION:
The Heart of the Matter

"Hear, O Israel, the Lord our God, the Lord is one. Love the
Lord your God with all your heart and with all your soul
and with all your mind and with all your strength."
—MARK 12:29–30

Parenting is a wondrous mystery, because on our children's birthdays God makes us stewards of tiny human beings who have unique personalities and a curious thing called a "free will." Each child has his own special way of coping with life and of expressing himself. Part of the wonderful mystery of parenting is discovering exactly who these little packages from heaven are!

I will never forget the thrill of holding each of my children for the first time. Even as newborn babies, their personalities differed. One rested in my arms and nursed contentedly. Another one raged at the trauma she had just been through, settled down for a moment, and then seemed to remember her birth and talk about it again. And our third child slept happily, demanding so little from us. Each of our children is a special treasure given to us by an all-knowing and loving God.

God gives us our children to parent, and He calls us to a high standard. In Mark 12:30, Jesus says, "Love the Lord your God with all your heart and with all your soul and with all your mind and with all your strength." Will we be faithful to raise our children in a way that they will desire to know God and seek Him with all their heart?

When God created Adam and Eve, He began this uncertain thing called humanity that would forever delight and disappoint Him. (Sounds a lot like parenting, doesn't it?) People often wonder why God—the author of all life and the sovereign God in control of all creation—wouldn't have chosen to "program" people to automatically make the right choices.

I'm sure the answer is much more complicated than this, but I think God loves us so much that He was willing to live with a fallen people who would continually make heartbreaking choices. Jesus said, "If you love Me, you'll keep My commandments" (see John 14:21). What kind of love would it be if obedience were an automated response rather than a choice? God has given us a free will so that we might freely will to love and obey Him with all our heart. To give us that choice is itself amazing love!

And, in God's goodness, He has given us children. From the day they enter our lives, children fill our hearts with love and, if we're totally honest, a small sense of dread. How in the world can we possibly be everything that our children need us to be? How will we ever make the right choices that shape our children to also make the right choices?

We realize, deep down, that even if we do come close to making the right choices, our children may not do the same. We can point to godly parents who serve God entirely and yet have prodigal children. What's that all about, we wonder. Where are the sure guarantees?

For years, Christian parents have clung to Proverbs 22:6, "Train a child in the way he should go, and when he is old he will not turn from it." See! There's the promise, parents say; if I do everything right, then my prodigal child will eventually come back to God!

Parents wait. And hope that they did everything right so their child will truly return. Some of these parents may even die clinging to their hope. And some parents waver under an extreme burden of guilt, wondering if they didn't do it "right." Where are the sure guarantees?

Proverbs 22:6 is not a sure guarantee. A problem with claiming this verse as a guaranteed truth is that we can't interpret a proverb as a promise. Biblical proverbs are considered to be truisms rather than promises from God. Yes, they are true, but they are not guarantees. What this proverb does say to us as parents is that we may do everything right and our children will still go astray, *but* they probably won't.

Is there a perfect plan for parenting then? Log onto the Internet or stop by any bookstore, and you'll find tons of plans, many of them very good, and some not so good. So many experts, each with a different plan—but whose plan is the best?

I look at parents who've gone before me and evaluate, so to speak, the fruit of their labor. Why are some parents more effective than others? Why do children in the same family sometimes turn out so differently? With the same parents, one of the children may love God and the other rejects Him. Is there any rhyme or reason?

The answers to these questions—if there were definitive answers—would wipe out every other parenting philosophy or strategy if they were known. My husband and I, like most other Christian parents, would pay big money and devote every free moment to getting those answers. We want to make the best parenting choices in those times when we have time to think about the choices, and also when the choices just seem to be thrust upon us in the heat of the moment. We would love to know that we are doing all the right things all the time. If only there were a clear path.

Is there a sure plan? Is it possible to raise our children in such a way that they love God with all their heart? The Word of God speaks authoritatively about parenting our children to love God with all their heart, all their soul, all their mind, and all their strength. Rather than suggesting that there's a perfect plan, let me just say at this point that the answer is not in methods, but in the mysteries of the heart—in your heart and your child's heart.

And who knows the heart better than God? Second Chronicles 6:30 is a prayer to God that clarifies this point: "Then hear from heaven, your dwelling place. Forgive, and deal with each man according to all he does, since you know his heart (for you alone know the hearts of men)." God alone knows our children's hearts, and He alone can give us the clues to understand these mysteries.

When they launch from our homes, we want our children to love God with all their heart. Mike and I are on a journey to discover what that means. And that is what this book, *With All Their Heart,* is about.

Welcome to this journey where I will tell stories from ours and others' sojourns. The chapters are short for the busiest people on the planet—parents. Dig into the Scriptures to allow the Holy Spirit to lead you into God's revelation of truth.

1

STRAIGHT TO
THE HEART

"Hear, O Israel: The LORD our God, the LORD is one. Love the LORD your
God with all your heart and with all your soul and with all your strength.
These commandments that I give you today are to be upon your hearts.
Impress them on your children. Talk about them when you sit at home and
when you walk along the road, when you lie down and when you get up."
—DEUTERONOMY 6:4–7

As a test, a lawyer asked Jesus, "Which is the greatest commandment?" Jesus could have answered anything.

"Be a good disciple."

"Do what's right."

"Don't sin."

"Give all your money to the poor, and come follow Me."

How would you have answered that question? How would we,
as parents, answer another question: What is the greatest commandment for our children?

Or . . .

Who do we hope our kids turn out to be?

Or . . .

What is the goal of our parenting?

Think about that last question, and don't turn the page until
you've answered it. Go ahead and write your answer in the box below.

The goal of parenting is . . .

What did you write as your goal for parenting? How much of your goal focuses on behavior or observable actions? How much focuses on attitudes or inward qualities?

Like most parents, your goal is probably a mixture of both. When Jesus was asked to give the greatest commandment, He said, "'Love the Lord your God with all your heart and with all your soul and with all your strength and with all your mind'; and, 'Love your neighbor as yourself'" (Luke 10:27).

Jesus focused on the inside and the outside. His primary focus was an inward love for God and others that results in outward observable actions. Jesus focused on the heart over and over in His conversations with people.

Yet how many of us as parents deal primarily with our children's actions rather than their hearts?

I know. I'm a mother of three, a full-time executive editor, an active team member in our church's children's ministry, an author, a wife, ad infinitum (or ad nauseum, at times). I know how it feels to be tired and have my children fussing about a toy that one of them won't share or not getting to go first or whatever the current crisis is. When my stamina is wearing down and all I'm thinking about is a good nap (for me), my initial reaction is to stop the voice that's irritating me. In our home, we sometimes call those grating tones the "whiney-boes." I just want to stop the kids' complaints with a rule, a punishment, or an instant apology from one of them.

I get what I want—in the moment—but I know that if I don't go deeper into my children's behavior to touch and shape their hearts, they will dutifully do what's necessary to navigate the rules of our household. And then when they move away from home, they'll do whatever they want.

That's simply not good enough!

I want my children to say "amen!" to what the psalmist says in Psalm 44:18, "Our hearts had not turned back; our feet had not strayed from your path."

That is a primary goal each of us must have for our children—that their hearts will never turn back from seeking God fully. Their career, their "success," whom they marry, the degrees they earn—even what they "do for God"—don't matter if they do not spend their lives seeking God with their whole heart.

Note that the interesting thing about Psalm 44:18 is that the position of the psalmist's heart preceded the action of his feet. He writes, "Our hearts had not turned back," and therefore "our feet had not strayed." It's heart first, actions second.

We have an amazing God-given responsibility and opportunity to shape our children's hearts in a way that causes their feet to stay on the path of seeking God with all their heart. Apart from God's grace and work in our children's hearts, this is not possible. But with God, all things are possible!

Set out on the wonderful adventure of being intentional in the way you parent your children so everything you do and say goes straight to their hearts.

Prayer for Today

God, I ask You to fill me with the knowledge of Your will through all spiritual wisdom and understanding. I pray that as a parent, I may live a life worthy of You and please You in every way: bearing fruit in every good work, growing in the knowledge of You. Amen.
Based on Colossians 1:9–10

Reflections

1. How close is your goal for parenting to the "greatest commandment"?
2. Do you agree or disagree that children loving God with all their heart should be the goal of your parenting? Explain.
3. How does your "amazing responsibility and opportunity to shape your children's hearts to seek God" make you feel? Explain.
4. Are there any obstacles in your heart that could keep you from receiving all that God wants you to get from this

book? If so, spend time getting right with God before you continue.

"I press on toward the goal to win the prize for which God has called me heavenward in Christ Jesus."

—*Philippians 3:14*

2

CARDIAC ARREST

Mendy Maserang told me that when her daughter Danee was three, she asked her mother if Jesus was in her heart. "Yes," Mendy replied.

Danee lay her head on her mother's chest, listened carefully, and said, "I think I can hear Him playing the drums."

What is the heart? Is it the physical organ where Jesus plays the bongos? The heart—the physical organ—is an amazing wonder created by God. It delivers life-giving blood to the entire body. If it's not functioning at its full capacity, the rest of the body pays for it. The physical organ, however, is not what we're talking about here.

The Hebrew word for heart is *kardia* (thus, the use of "cardiac" to refer to the heart in modern language). Originally, according to W. E. Vine, *kardia* referred to the "chief organ of physical life that occupies the most important place" in the body. Early on, though, the word transitioned to mean the figurative heart that encompasses the emotions (what we feel), the mind (what we think), and the will (what we choose). The heart is so much more than the physical organ when it's mentioned in Scripture. Vine writes that "the heart is used figuratively for the hidden springs of the personal life."

When I was a child, I trekked up to the headwaters of a mountain spring with my aunt and uncle. They went there each spring to gather wild watercress that flourished in the cool spring waters, and this time they invited my siblings and me to come along. We began down by the ice-cold Dill Creek that fed into the red clay-bound waters of the Washita River. We hiked upstream by the creek—long enough for us kids to lose our fascination with the outdoors.

Finally, we found the clear cool waters surging from a small hill. We had found the hidden springs of Dill Creek, whose water droplets eventually mingled with the Washita River that ultimately flowed into the ocean—such a great journey for such a small spring. And to think that the great rivers of the world have their beginning in something so small and seemingly insignificant.

That's the way it is with the heart. Proverbs 4:23 challenges us: "Above all else, guard your heart, for it is the wellspring of life." Just as the world's oceans find their source in the mighty rivers that are fed by creeks and ultimately springs, so our life finds its source in our heart. Everything I feel, think, and choose ultimately shapes and creates my life. Who I am begins in the figurative heart within me.

Proverbs 27:19 says, "As water reflects a face, so a man's heart reflects the man." Anything we see in a person's life has its starting place in that person's heart—in the person's mind, will, and emotions. For example, Cindy and Doug, two teenagers struggling with sexual immorality, asked an older Christian woman to hold them accountable. Each week, they met to pray and discuss how the week went. Things got better, but the couple still struggled with their sin. Finally, one day, Cindy acknowledged to Catherine that she had spent years reading pornographic romance novels before she and Doug had ever met. A pattern of fantasizing about sex in her heart had made it much easier for her to make the transition to actually committing the sin. And because Cindy's heart was full of lust, stopping the act was made even more difficult. Cindy needed to deal with not just her actions, but her heart, before she could genuinely repent and change.

Consider these verses (italics added) that reveal that the heart is the starting place for everything in our life:

"Then your *heart* will become proud and you will forget the LORD your God, who brought you out of Egypt, out of the land of slavery." (Deuteronomy 8:14) *(A proud heart leads to forgetting God.)*

"I know, my God, that you test the *heart* and are pleased with integrity." (1 Chronicles 29:17) *(Integrity flows from the heart.)*

"Not a word from their mouth can be trusted; their *heart* is filled with destruction. Their throat is an open grave; with their tongue they speak deceit." (Psalm 5:9) *(A destruction-filled heart results in untrustworthy and destructive words.)*

"Their deeds do not permit them to return to their God. A spirit of prostitution is in their *heart;* they do not acknowledge the LORD." (Hosea 5:4) *(An unfaithful, promiscuous heart turns away from God.)*

"Their *hearts* are like an oven; they approach him with intrigue. Their passion smolders all night; in the morning it blazes like a flaming fire." (Hosea 7:6) *(The heart cooks up trouble before the act is ever done.)*

"But the things that come out of the mouth come from the *heart,* and these make a man 'unclean.' For out of the *heart* come evil thoughts, murder, adultery, sexual immorality, theft, false testimony, slander." (Matthew 15:18–19) *(It's not behavior that affects the heart, Jesus says; it's the heart that affects behavior.)*

"You brood of vipers, how can you who are evil say anything good? For out of the overflow of the *heart* the mouth speaks." (Matthew 12:34) *(Our words come directly from our hearts.)*

"'The pride of your *heart* has deceived you, you who live in the clefts of the rocks and make your home on the heights, you who say to yourself, "Who can bring me down to the ground?" Though you soar like the eagle and make your nest among the stars, from there I will bring you down,' declares the LORD." (Obadiah 1:3–4) *(A proud heart deceives us.)*

"Then Peter said, 'Ananias, how is it that Satan has so filled your *heart* that you have lied to the Holy Spirit and have kept for yourself some of the money you received for the land?'" (Acts 5:3) *(Satan's work in a human heart leads a person to sin.)*

So that you don't become discouraged in your quest to help your children love God with all their heart, consider these verses that illustrate how good things flow out of our hearts as well.

"Tell the Israelites to bring me an offering. You are to receive the offering for me from each man whose *heart* prompts him to give." (Exodus 25:2) *(Acts of generosity flow from the heart.)*

"Then Hezekiah said, 'You have now dedicated yourselves to the LORD. Come and bring sacrifices and thank offerings to the temple of the LORD.' So the assembly brought sacrifices and thank offerings, and all whose *hearts* were willing brought burnt offerings." (2 Chronicles 29:31) *(Willing hearts result in service and gratitude to God.)*

"Rend your *heart* and not your garments. Return to the LORD your God, for he is gracious and compassionate, slow to anger and abounding in love, and he relents from sending calamity." (Joel 2:13) *(Repentance must begin in the heart, not in actions.)*

"For where your treasure is, there your *heart* will be also." (Matthew 6:21) *(Where we invest our time and money, our hearts follow. Or, perhaps, where our hearts are, our time and money follow.)*

"The sacrifices of God are a broken spirit; a broken and contrite *heart,* O God, you will not despise." (Psalm 51:17) *(God loves a humble heart.)*

"That if you confess with your mouth, 'Jesus is Lord,' and believe in your *heart* that God raised him from the dead, you will be saved. For it is with your *heart* that you believe and are justified, and it is with your mouth that you confess and are saved." (Romans 10:9–10) *(Justification requires a believing heart.)*

If we're going to parent our children to give them every opportunity to love God with all their heart, we need to understand that life flows from the heart. It is always heart first, and then actions.

Prayer for Today

God, because everything flows from our hearts, I pray that You will help my children be pure in heart. Thank You, God, that You will bless their pure hearts and allow them to see You. Amen.

Based on Matthew 5:8

Reflections

1. Explain the connectedness of these three things in the heart: feelings, thoughts, and choices.
2. In your life, how have you seen your heart shape your life?
3. Think about each of your children. What does each child's outward attitudes and actions reveal about his or her heart?

4. Consider any not-so-lovely things you've discovered about the heart of each of your children. What does God's Word say about that area?

"I have chosen the way of truth; I have set my heart on your laws. I hold fast to your statutes, O LORD; do not let me be put to shame."

—*Psalm 119:30–31*

3
HEART OF
THE GOSPEL

*"One of those listening was a woman named Lydia, a dealer in
purple cloth from the city of Thyatira, who was a worshiper of
God. The Lord opened her heart to respond to Paul's message."*
—ACTS 16:14

Francis Thompson wrote a poem that refers to God as the
"Hound of Heaven." I remember the first time I read that poem.
I immediately understood what that term meant, because I had
experienced God hunting for me all my life.

My family didn't attend church often when I was young, but
for some reason the little white church at the bottom of the hill
in Morenci, Arizona, beckoned to me. I begged to go to that
church.

My mother dressed me for church one Sunday and loaded my
older brother and sister in the car with me. She dropped me off
at the church and says she remembers sitting sheepishly in the car
as I tried to open the door. I was too small to even reach the door
handle.

"Get out and help your sister," she told my pajama-clad brother. He wasn't budging, and neither was anyone else in the car. Finally, an older gentleman approached the church and opened the door to let me into this place that called to my soul. My mother says that the next Sunday the entire family went to church.

Later, at the age of four, I attended my first vacation Bible school, where I heard the heart of the gospel explained clearly for the first time. Jesus had died for me! I wanted desperately to give my life to this Jesus who loved me.

After many of us children responded to the gospel message, the pastor took us into his office. The pastor wanted each of us to tell why we wanted to receive Jesus Christ as our Savior. To this day, I vividly remember sitting in a circle with a dozen other children. Each child told why he or she had responded, and my turn was winding around the circle. I can't remember what anyone else said except for my best friend, Debbie. "I have to get glasses this week," was her reason.

And then it was my turn. "I want to give my life to Jesus," I said with as much excitement as I could muster to convince this pastor that I was worthy.

When it was all said and done, he deemed all of us as "not ready yet." I left that church unsaved and returned to my unchurched family.

Yet the Hound of Heaven still sought me.

Three years later at a small country church in Oklahoma, I walked the aisle to say that I believed in Jesus Christ. My sister, Terryl, did, too. We were baptized in Dill Creek while our small, elderly congregation stood on the banks and sang, "Shall We Gather at the River?"

I had no discipleship after that because I didn't attend church regularly. Once in Sunday school during this time, the children prayed for things they were thankful for—the trees, the flowers, their pets. At the end, they said, "In Jesus' name. Amen."

In my heart, I decided I would never say "in Jesus' name." *I am never going to say that,* I thought, and I didn't.

I had responded to the heart of the gospel, but I had not allowed the gospel to change my heart. My life was anything but a Christian life.

By the time I was nineteen, I was depressed and hopeless. All the things I had believed would fill my emptiness had only made me emptier.

At that time, my sister gave me a book about a man who had had everything but had not found true happiness until he lost everything and found Jesus. I prayed to God and said, "If You are real, I want You to tell me—not to hear it from people!"

I started reading the Bible—sometimes in secret so my roommates wouldn't know. I read Matthew, Mark, Luke, and John. The Hound of Heaven made His presence evident to me.

Once I remember driving in my Ford Pinto and feeling as though God's presence was hovering over my car. "What do You want?!" I cried out. Anything I read or listened to seemed always to have a message about God in it. I could not get away from Him.

One night while camping and reading my Bible by candlelight, I read a verse that cut right to my heart. It was John 16:24: "Until now you have not asked for anything in my name. Ask and you will receive, and your joy will be complete."

I had forgotten the promise I had made to myself not to pray in Jesus' name, but I could almost see myself as a little girl in that Sunday school room at that moment. And here was the God of the universe saying that He knew what I had said. I realized that if God knew that, then He knew everything about me, and He knew I could never be truly happy without Him.

I prayed, "Jesus, please come into my life and make me happy. In Jesus' name."

Since all of my church experiences were as a child, the only thing I knew to do was sing. And the only song I knew to sing was "This Little Light of Mine." I sang that, and my candlelight seemed to become a torch as God penetrated my heart.

I understand that God is a relentless "hound" who hunts us down with His love, His kindness, and His favor. I'm so grateful that God pursued me and that, in the same way, He is pursuing my children with the heart of the gospel—His heart!

I love 1 Corinthians 15:3–4 because it so clearly captures the heart of the gospel: "For what I received I passed on to you as of first importance: that Christ died for our sins according to the Scriptures, that he was buried, that he was raised on the third day according to the Scriptures."

That's good news! We have the greatest news to tell a dark and dying world that apart from Christ knows only emptiness. As Christian parents, we have this news to tell the children God has sovereignly placed in our lives. God longs for our children to come to a saving faith in Him—even more than we long for them to make that decision.

In Acts 15:7–9, Peter addressed the Jewish leadership of the church regarding the salvation of the Gentiles.

> After much discussion, Peter got up and addressed them: "Brothers, you know that some time ago God made a choice among you that the Gentiles might hear from my lips the message of the gospel and believe. God, who knows the heart, showed that he accepted them by giving the Holy Spirit to them, just as he did to us. He made no distinction between us and them, for he purified their hearts by faith."

God has made a choice that our children hear the message of the gospel, most likely from our lips. And God will lovingly accept our children and purify their hearts by faith when they believe. Although their response is not a guarantee, our telling them the good news is not optional; it's our duty as Christian parents.

Because our children are depending on us to take them by the hand and lead them along the path of life, we need to clearly explain the heart of the gospel to them. Our children need their hearts purified by faith in Christ first of all. Once they receive God's forgiveness for sins, they'll receive the same Holy Spirit that we adults receive upon faith in Christ.

It is only by God's Holy Spirit at work in our children's hearts that they can come to know God and follow Him wholeheartedly. This must be our most fervent prayer for each of our children.

As you share the message of the gospel with your children, remember these practical tips to communicate clearly with them.

• **Use concrete terminology.** Perhaps the metaphor children can most understand is that of a family. Avoid using "ask Jesus into your heart"; this conjures up all sorts of images in a child's head and truly isn't accurate theology. Instead, emphasize that God wants to "become our heavenly Father." Your child will more clearly understand that God wants to adopt him into His family and make him His child.

• **Enter into a dialogue with your child.** Tell what God has done in your life and how you became a Christian. As you explain that God gave us the special gift of Jesus to forgive our sins, stop to ask clarifying questions. Ask open-ended (not "yes" or "no") questions so you truly understand your child's grasp of what you're saying.

• **Celebrate your child's decision.** Although sanctification is a process, for a child to be able to point to the day that he or she received Christ as Savior is a powerful faith marker. In our home, we've celebrated by throwing a born-again birthday party, complete with a birthday cake. Write the date in your child's Bible, then celebrate the anniversary of your child's most important decision each year.

Prayer for Today

God, I pray that I may be active in discussing my faith with my children—not only so that I will have a full understanding of every good thing that is in our lives in Christ, but so they will as well. I pray that my love for my children and for You will give great joy and encouragement to my family—and that having You in our home will refresh each of our hearts. Amen.

Based on Philemon 6–7

Reflections

1. Does each of your children have a personal relationship with Jesus Christ? If so, when did that happen? If not, when would be a good time to discuss the heart of the gospel with your children?
2. How would you explain the gospel to your children? If you're not sure, with whom could you discuss this to learn how?
3. What difference has your faith in Christ made in your heart?
4. Spend time praying for the salvation and spiritual growth of each of your children.

"Consequently, faith comes from hearing the message, and the message is heard through the word of Christ."

—Romans 10:17

4
GOD'S WORK IN HEARTS

"I am the vine; you are the branches. If a man remains in me and I in him, he will bear much fruit; apart from me you can do nothing."

—JOHN 15:5

A few summers ago during our vacation to Oklahoma, we traded in our broken-down van for a used Suburban. It was beautiful, and we were thrilled to have gotten a great deal on it.

The day we were supposed to head back to Colorado, we heard a strange noise coming from the Suburban. Only twenty miles from my parents' home, we turned around, rather than risk getting stranded on the side of the road.

It turned out, though, that the noise was simply the luggage rack on top of our new Suburban; we hadn't accounted for the fact that it would make a different noise on this vehicle when the wind blew under it. We were a little embarrassed, but time had slipped away, so we stayed another day.

On our return trip, just over the Colorado border, Mike was

driving 75 mph when our right rear wheel flew off—the entire thing! I cried out "Jesus, take control!" and then watched Mike handle our car as though he were a professional driver. We careened from left to right for a mile, at one time hurtling toward a ravine. My ten-year-old son Grant and I cried out to God at each turn.

By the time our vehicle came to a halt on the side of the road, we were filled with a peace that we knew could come only from God. We weren't sure what had happened until we climbed out of the car. A mother and her adult daughter who were following us had already pulled over before we got out of the car.

"Are you OK?" they asked as they embraced us. "That was the most amazing thing I've ever seen!" the mother, Faith, exclaimed.

After assessing the damage and calling a tow truck, Mike had Faith take Abby, Reed, and me to a small town a few miles back. Once there, I kept telling my children, "God saved us!"

We prayed together and thanked God for His protection and for saving our family. We realized that it was only the hand of God that had saved us from destruction.

Later, we discovered that had we been on the highway the day before, we would have been in a rainstorm. Controlling the car on slick roads would have been even more difficult. God had protected us by keeping us off the road the day before.

In this situation, there was a sense of us being out of control, but of God being in control. We were helpless to help ourselves. Without God's help, the end of this situation would have been very different.

In many ways, that's what parenting is like. We may feel like we're in control, but, ultimately, only God is in control. Yes, God calls us to be faithful to the things that He has revealed to us— just as Mike had to hang onto the steering wheel. We are not to throw up our hands and just expect God to keep us on the right path.

Yet, without the work of God in our children's hearts, all of our efforts to train our children and help shape their hearts to love God are worthless. God has called us to be partners with Him in parenting our children. Psalm 127:1 says, "Unless the LORD builds the house, its builders labor in vain. Unless the LORD watches over the city, the watchmen stand guard in vain."

And Jesus said in John 6:44, "No one can come to me unless the Father who sent me draws him." We are totally and completely dependent on God to work in our children's hearts.

So what does Scripture reveal about the work of God in our hearts? In the rest of this chapter, we'll take a look at what God does in our children's hearts, with each verse followed by the most appropriate response to such truth—prayer.

• God knows our hearts

"If we had forgotten the name of our God or spread out our hands to a foreign god, would not God have discovered it, since he knows the secrets of the heart?" (Psalm 44:20–21)

God, You know my children's hearts. You know their secrets and the hidden things that I will never know. Father, guide my children in the secret places of their hearts. Shine Your light in their hearts—and drive away any darkness. Help my children to live their lives with the knowledge that You know their hearts.

• God purifies our hearts by faith

"God, who knows the heart, showed that he accepted them by giving the Holy Spirit to them, just as he did to us. He made no distinction between us and them, for he purified their hearts by faith." (Acts 15:8–9)

God, I pray that You would help my children to accept Christ as their Savior and to grow in You. Please remove anything that stands in the way of their salvation. And I thank You that You will accept them by giving them Your Holy Spirit. God, purify their hearts by faith.

• God searches our hearts

"I the LORD search the heart and examine the mind, to reward a man according to his conduct, according to what his deeds deserve." (Jeremiah 17:10)

God, search my children's hearts and examine their minds. Lead them in the way where their conduct will be pleasing to You. Thank You, God, that You will reward my children's deeds of obedience. And even more, God, thank You that You put it in their hearts to want to do good.

• God tests our hearts

"Remember how the LORD your God led you all the way in the desert these forty years, to humble you and to test you in order to know what was in your heart, whether or not you would keep his commands." (Deuteronomy 8:2)

God, I pray that You would test my children's hearts and that You would help them to know that You are so interested in what's in their hearts. I pray that You would give my children the heart to obey You completely.

• God hardens/softens hearts

"Then the LORD said to Moses, 'Go to Pharaoh, for I have hardened his heart and the hearts of his officials so that I may perform these miraculous signs of mine among them that you may tell your children and grandchildren how I dealt harshly with the Egyptians and how I performed my signs among them, and that you may know that I am the LORD.'" (Exodus 10:1–2)

God, I know that You hardened Pharaoh's heart so You could reveal Yourself to Your people and the unbelieving Egyptians. And I know that Your plans for my children to glorify You are far above anything I can even imagine. Yet I pray, God, that You will keep my children's hearts soft toward You. Protect them from hardening their hearts.

• God writes His law on our hearts

"'This is the covenant I will make with the house of Israel after that time,' declares the LORD. 'I will put my law in their minds and write it on their hearts. I will be their God, and they will be my people.'" (Jeremiah 31:33)

God, I pray that You would make my children's hearts to be tablets that have Your Word written on them. Lord, help them to not only know Your Word, but also to have it inscribed deeply within them.

• God puts His Spirit in our hearts

"Now it is God who makes both us and you stand firm in Christ. He anointed us, set his seal of ownership on us, and put his Spirit in our hearts as a deposit, guaranteeing what is to come." (2 Corinthians 1:21–22)

God, thank You that You are not a God who is far off, but You are up close and personal. I thank You that as my children believe in the message of Jesus' death and resurrection, You put Your Spirit in their hearts. I pray for my children that they will be sensitive to the Spirit's promptings within their hearts.

• God pours out His love in our hearts

"And hope does not disappoint us, because God has poured out his love into our hearts by the Holy Spirit, whom he has given us." (Romans 5:5)

God, I pray that You would fill my children with the hope that does not disappoint. I pray that You would pour out Your love into their hearts by Your Holy Spirit.

• God gives us hearts to know Him

"I will give them a heart to know me, that I am the LORD. They will be my people, and I will be their God, for they will return to me with all their heart." (Jeremiah 24:7)

God, I pray that You would give my children hearts to know You. I pray that my children will be Your people and that You will be their God. I pray that they will turn to You with all their hearts.

• God circumcises our hearts

"The LORD your God will circumcise your hearts and the hearts of your descendants, so that you may love him with all your heart and with all your soul, and live." (Deuteronomy 30:6)

God, I thank You that You alone are the One who can circumcise hearts. I thank You that circumcision is a sign of being set apart. I pray that You will set apart my children's hearts to love You completely and entirely.

• God gives an undivided heart

"I will give them an undivided heart and put a new spirit in them; I will remove from them their heart of stone and give them a heart of flesh. Then they will follow my decrees and be careful to keep my laws. They will be my people, and I will be their God." (Ezekiel 11:19–20)

God, I pray that You will give my children undivided hearts and put a new spirit in them. Remove from them any hardness of heart, and instead give them soft hearts. Help them to follow Your decrees and be careful to keep Your laws. Let them be Your people, and be their God.

Prayer for Today

God, I pray that my children will not only hear but also understand Your truths; that they will not only see but also perceive all that You have for them. Protect their hearts from becoming calloused, their ears from becoming deaf, and their eyes from becoming blind.

Lord, help them to understand You with their hearts and turn from any wicked ways so that You may heal them. Amen.

Based on Acts 28:26–27

Reflections

1. Why is prayer the "most appropriate response" to these Scriptures?
2. How do you feel knowing that God plays a role in your children's hearts?
3. Which of the above truths about what God does in your children's hearts mean the most to you? Explain.
4. Think of an area of struggle with your children. Which of the above truths about God speak to that issue? How can knowing that God is able to work in your children's hearts in that area make a difference in your situation?

"Death and Destruction lie open before the LORD—how much more the hearts of men!"

—Proverbs 15:11

5

LIKE MIGHTY WARRIORS

"My little children, let us not love in word or in tongue,
but in deed and in truth."

—I JOHN 3:18 NKJV

It had been a particularly stressful day. I don't even remember why, but I wasn't dealing well with the stress. That day, I had taken it out on my husband. I was discouraged and disturbed that I had acted in such an unchristian manner to Mike—and in front of Grant.

On the way to run one more errand, four-year-old Grant asked me, "Mommy, do you love God?"

What do I answer? I wondered. I quickly reviewed my options.

I could say yes and have him think that I am the biggest hypocrite who ever lived after the way I'd acted that day. Or, I could say no and have him think that I'm not even a Christian.

Rather than answering his question simply by saying something like, "Yes, I love God, but sometimes I do things that make Him sad, and I have to tell Him I'm sorry," I started giving him a complicated answer. "Well, I'd have to say by the way I've acted today that it doesn't *seem* like I love God. Because if I loved God, I would . . ."

My voice trailed off as I heard quiet little sobs coming from my precious child. I looked over at him. He was slumped against his car door, gently quaking as he cried.

I reached out to him. "What's wrong, Grant? What is it?"

Through his tears, he choked out, "You make me feel like you're saying that you love the devil."

Of course that wasn't what I was saying—or was it? In Grant's childlike way, he illustrated Jesus' words when He said, "You're either with Me or against Me."

There's a temptation for us as parents to let the church take care of our children's Christian education. Yet the truth is that every single hour of the day, our children are getting an education from us—whether it's Christian or not!

In Deuteronomy 6:4–9, God says to parents:

Hear, O Israel: The LORD our God, the LORD is one. Love the LORD your God with all your heart and with all your soul and with all your strength. These commandments that I give you today are to be upon your hearts. Impress them on your children. Talk about them when you sit at home and when you walk along the road, when you lie down and when you get up. Tie them as symbols on your hands and bind them on your foreheads. Write them on the doorframes of your houses and on your gates.

As much as I believe in Christian education for children at church, there's no mention here of children's ministry, Sunday school, children's church, or any other church children's program. Does that mean that they're wrong? Absolutely not.

The charge in Deuteronomy 6 does mean, though, that the primary Christian educators of children are parents, not children's ministers. I am grateful for the partnership of wonderful people in my church who minister to all three of my children. I am one of those people who ministers to my own—and others'—children through our children's ministry.

I believe, though, that as great as our children's ministry is, my children will not fully understand the truths they're learning if they don't see them lived out and practiced on a day-to-day basis at home. Do we do it perfectly every single day? No way. Not even every single hour! Yet, even in that there's a lesson about God's grace and forgiveness.

God's Word is clear about parents' responsibility to help their children love God with all their heart. And it's clear about the benefits to our children when we ourselves love God with all our heart!

Zechariah 10:7 says that because of what parents do, "their children will see it and be joyful; their hearts will rejoice in the LORD." What could make children rejoice? The answer to that is in Zechariah 10:5–9 where God describes the victorious Ephraimites.

• **God at work**—Verse 6 says, "I will strengthen the house of Judah and save the house of Joseph. I will restore them because I have compassion on them. They will be as though I had not rejected them, for I am the LORD their God and I will answer them." Our children need to see that God is at work in our lives. The truth is that for our children to see our living faith, they need to see results, such as a vital love relationship with God, His power in our lives, and answers to prayer.

• **Power and joy**—Verse 7 says, "The Ephraimites will become like mighty men, and their hearts will be glad as with wine. Their children will see it and be joyful; their hearts will rejoice in the LORD." Again, our children need to see the power of God in our lives and ministries. They also need to see overflowing joy—even as though we are drunk—in our relationship with God.

41

The amazing result of these three things is that our children will rejoice because of what the Lord has done through us. That's a worthy goal! The example of a parent who loves God with all his or her heart is one of the most powerful tools God can use to shape a child's heart.

Two years ago, twelve-year-old Josh Kamrath hated singing at church. In fact his mother, Carmen, says that he was a downright pill about it.

Carmen remembers, though, when things changed for Josh. The Kamrath family took worship CDs from their church on a road trip. Not only did they listen to the CDs, but they worshiped with them. Dan Kamrath drove and sang, worshiping God with all his heart. Before long, Carmen turned around and saw Josh and her two girls singing worshipfully.

"To see him excited and on fire to worship is such a blessing now," Carmen says. "I think it's because he needed the right motivation and example. By seeing his dad fully worship and love it, he's now motivated to sing at church."

Psalm 112:1–9 also stresses the importance of parents' righteousness. Verse 2 says that the righteous person's children will be "mighty in the land." What is it that the righteous person does as listed in this psalm? Here's the litany of things this righteous person possesses . . .

- Fear of the Lord,
- Delight in God's commands,
- Graciousness,
- Compassion,
- Generosity,
- Justice,
- A steadfast heart that trusts in the Lord,
- No fear, and
- Triumph over his enemies.

As we possess these things and are growing in them, our children will automatically know the answer to the question: "Mommy (or Daddy), do you love God?"

Prayer for Today

God, I long to be effective and productive in my knowledge of the Lord Jesus Christ and in my children's faith development. For this reason, help these things to be present and growing in my life: faith, goodness, knowledge, self-control, perseverance, godliness, brotherly kindness, and love. Amen.

Based on 2 Peter 1:5–8

Reflections

1. How would you answer the question, "Do you love God?"
2. How would your actions answer the question, "Do you love God?"
3. Consider whether you've defaulted your role as your children's primary Christian educator to your church. If so, what changes do you need to make?
4. If you were tried in a court, what evidence would there be to the living presence of God in your life?
5. Which things are present in your life from the list in Psalm 112?
6. What is God calling you to do differently in order to be the example for your children that you need to be?

"You are the salt of the earth. But if the salt loses its saltiness, how can it be made salty again? It is no longer good for anything, except to be thrown out and trampled by men.

"You are the light of the world. A city on a hill cannot be hidden. Neither do people light a lamp and put it under a bowl. Instead they put it on its stand, and it gives light to everyone in the house. In the same way, let your light shine before men, that they may see your good deeds and praise your Father in heaven."

—Matthew 5:13–16

6
TAKING
NAMES

"Then Peter came to Jesus and asked, 'Lord, how many times shall I forgive my brother when he sins against me? Up to seven times?' Jesus answered, 'I tell you, not seven times, but seventy-seven times.'"
—MATTHEW 18:21–22

One day after school when he was seven, Grant came home out of sorts. He fought with Abby and overreacted to my correction. He plopped down at the top of the stairs and gave me a hateful look.

"Just don't talk to me," he demanded in the middle of my correction.

That stance and those words are usually "fightin' words" for me. How dare he shut me off in the middle of my discipline? But on this day I felt a load of grace dumped on me.

"Why don't you go to your room and spend some time alone?" I said. "You're not in trouble, but I think you just need to be alone."

Without a word, he went to his room.

Ten minutes later, I walked by with our eight-month-old son and set him just inside Grant's room. "Watch him, and don't let him get into anything," I requested and went on to the bathroom.

I returned to find that Grant had scooted over by Reed and was playing with him. I could tell by Grant's countenance that he was softening, but his body language warned me not to enter his room. So I sat in the hallway.

"How was your day?" I asked.

"Not good," he said. "The older girls chased me and Steven isn't my best friend anymore," he blurted out.

"Why?"

"He helped the girls, and he got some grass and he stuffed it in my mouth."

"Well, maybe you need to find some new friends," I said. How dare this boy mess with my son!

"Well, Chris and Ashlyn and Zach were trying to help me," he said.

"See, you have some good friends," I encouraged him. "Did you tell the playground teacher about this?"

"Yes, but she didn't do anything."

Soon, Grant had scooted over and was sitting next to me as we talked about what a rotten day he'd had.

Later that week, he had friend problems again.

"People call me names at school," he told Mike and me.

"What names?" I asked. He told me and then said that they didn't bug him too much.

"Good for you, Grant," Mike encouraged.

"Who calls you names?" I probed.

"I don't think it matters, Chris, as long as he's dealing with it," Mike said.

Didn't matter? Didn't matter? I was taking names! I wanted to know who was being mean to my little boy when I wasn't around to protect him. I wanted action.

The next day, driving to McDonald's Playland, I felt that old familiar nudge from the Holy Spirit. "You're not teaching your children to respond in Christlike ways," I sensed the Holy Spirit saying.

What? You mean my "taking names/change your friends" approach isn't the best? Instantly, I knew it wasn't.

After lunch in the noisy Playland area, three-year-old Abby came up to me, hands on hips, angry eyes, and pouty lips. "Them boys are being mean to me!" she complained because she wasn't getting her way.

I leaned over, looked in her eyes, and said, "Well, you just need to forgive them."

I could see an element of surprise because I didn't want to know *which* boys were being mean. She paused for a moment and then turned happily to take another run through the tunnel while I kept a watchful eye on her.

It's not easy to model forgiveness for our children, is it? Sometimes, it's not easy to forgive at all. Yet God demands it of us.

In Matthew 18, Jesus told the story of the unforgiving servant. Although forgiven of his debts, this servant was cruel and showed no mercy to those who owed him money. And that kind of unforgiveness results in the same kind of unforgiveness from God. In verse 35, Jesus says, "This is how my heavenly Father will treat each of you unless you forgive your brother from your heart."

How many times a day in your parenting do you have to deal with issues of forgiveness? The number of times is roughly parallel to the amount of time your children are together (that's not scientific; that's just my experience!). Our kids are going to fight, irritate one another, offend one another, and stand in need of forgiveness, just as we often stand in need of their forgiveness.

Jesus says in Matthew 6:14–15 that our forgiving others is a mandate for God forgiving us. He said, "For if you forgive men when they sin against you, your heavenly Father will also forgive you. But if you do not forgive men their sins, your Father will not forgive your sins."

A quick "I'm sorry" and an easy "I forgive you" may be genuine at times, but it may also be a formula that our children learn to use simply to end the discipline process. But short-circuiting the forgiveness process will never really affect their hearts. The practical application to leading our children to forgive one another is found in Colossians 3:12–15:

> Therefore, as God's chosen people, holy and dearly loved, clothe yourselves with compassion, kindness, humility, gentleness and patience. Bear with each other and forgive whatever grievances you may have against one another. Forgive as the Lord forgave you. And over all these virtues put on love, which binds them all together in perfect unity. Let the peace of Christ rule in your hearts, since as members of one body you were called to peace. And be thankful.

Verse 12 lists the things that we need to help our children develop toward one another so they are able to do what we are commanded in verse 13, which is to "bear with each other and forgive." Verse 12 tells us to have compassion, kindness, humility, gentleness, and patience. Let's define these terms in ways our kids can understand to help clarify what we're talking about. Here's what each of these things may sound like.

• **Compassion**—"I care about you. I'm sad when you're sad or hurt."

• **Kindness**—"I don't want to do anything to hurt you or make you sad. I want to help you and be your friend."

• **Humility**—"I am not more important than you are."

• **Gentleness**—"I will move toward you in my actions and speech in a way that is not harmful to you."

• **Patience**—"I understand that you are not perfect and that you are growing."

A look at other verses that contain this litany of heart attitudes reveals even more. Galatians 5:22–23 lists the fruit of the Spirit as "love, joy, peace, patience, kindness, goodness, faithfulness, gentleness and self-control." Since it's the fruit of the Spirit, these things are not fully possible without the presence of the Spirit of God in a child's life. Yet they are attitudes to nurture in all of our children. Even our children who have a personal relationship with Christ need to be encouraged and trained in these attitudes.

Ephesians 4:31–32 encourages children of God to "get rid of all bitterness, rage and anger, brawling and slander, along with every form of malice," and to instead "be kind and compassionate to one another, forgiving each other, just as in Christ God forgave you."

The motivation in the Ephesians passage and the Colossians passage is a response to what Christ has done for us. We are to pattern our life after Christ. In fact, in Ephesians 5:1–2, the Bible says that we are to be imitators of God. We are to teach our children to move toward one another in words and actions in the same way that Jesus Christ moves toward us—with compassion, kindness, humility, gentleness, and patience.

The truth is that the more our children get to know Jesus, the more they'll want to be like Him. That is one of the ultimate heart motivations for all our actions—to be like Christ.

I've found that the best way for children to develop these loving heart attitudes toward one another is to direct them into having empathy for one another. You can do this by following a procedure similar to this one. When there is an offense committed, give the offended child time to talk about her feelings. Or ask the offender how her actions may have made the other child feel. Or ask how the offender would have felt if she had been the offended one.

Use these simple questions:

• To the offended child: "How do you feel about what just happened?"

• To the offender: "How do you think your actions made your brother feel?" or "How would you have felt if someone had done this to you?"

Get to the feeling level so children can understand the true nature of their offense. As you help your children develop empathy and compassionate feelings for one another, they will then be able to "bear with" others and "forgive whatever grievances [they] may have against one another" (Colossians 3:13). And the amazing result for your family, from verse 15, is an overwhelming peace!

Prayer for Today

God, being in relationship with You is more than an intellectual exercise. So I pray that You will touch my children's hearts, so they can know Your presence. Help them to not become dependent on their feelings, but I pray that their relationship with You will be vibrant because You touch their hearts. Amen.

Based on 1 Samuel 10:26

Reflections

1. Is there anyone in your life whom you need to forgive? If so, what is standing in the way of your forgiving that person?
2. What makes forgiveness so difficult at times for you? For your children?
3. Which of the following do each of your children need the most growth in: compassion, kindness, humility, gentleness, or patience?

4. What are ways you can help your children develop empathy for one another?

"For if you forgive men when they sin against you, your heavenly Father will also forgive you."

—*Matthew 6:14*

7

JUST PASSING THROUGH

"Trust in the LORD with all your heart and lean not on your own understanding; in all your ways acknowledge him, and he will make your paths straight."
—PROVERBS 3:5–6

Alysia Kamrath was born with a rare bladder disorder. Every doctor who treated her said that he had never seen or heard of a case like hers. Alysia dealt with the pain of chronic cystitis and a partially paralyzed bladder every day of her life.

When Alysia went in for her fourth surgery, her parents, Dan and Carmen, sat in the waiting room, praying and waiting for some word about how she was doing. After only one hour, the anesthesiologist came to tell them the doctor would be out to speak with them shortly.

"Of course, we panicked!" Carmen said, because the surgery was scheduled to take three hours and seeing the anesthesiologist out of the operating room was a bit unnerving. "The doctor told us that the pocket they were going to remove from Alysia's bladder was no longer there," Carmen said. "We couldn't believe it!"

Alysia was in recovery when her parents first got to see her. When they told her what had happened, at first she was groggy and reacted with anger. "Why didn't they remove it?" she demanded. As she became more alert, though, her parents were able to explain what had happened.

Carmen said, "We were still very reluctant to believe it ourselves. We were afraid the doctors were missing something. We had seen the X-rays that showed the pocket, and we knew how many problems it had been causing for Alysia."

Alysia didn't need any verification of the miracle. She matter-of-factly looked at her parents and said, "God made a miracle for me!"

"If only we had faith that responded that quickly," Carmen said. "It took Dan and me a whole day for it to finally sink in that that's what it was—a miracle!"

Jesus calls us to have the kind of faith Alysia has—unquestioning and not requiring proof.

In Luke 24 after Jesus had been crucified, the disciples were desperately trying to figure out what had just happened to them. All the disciples' hopes had gone deep inside a tomb, and the stone had in essence been rolled to shut up their faith. Or so they thought.

The resurrected Jesus—incognito—had joined a couple of His disciples as they walked along the road. They began to tell Him everything that had happened. Finally, Jesus could take their confused ramblings no more. He said in Luke 24:25, "How foolish you are, and how slow of heart to believe all that the prophets have spoken!"

Jesus rebuked them for their lack of faith. They were slow of heart, He said. And a lack of faith is one of the things that grieves God more than anything else.

How can we help our children to not be slow of heart but have hearts that are quick to believe?

First of all, we have to define faith. Hebrews 11:1 says, "Now faith is being sure of what we hope for and certain of what we do not see." Faith is an assurance of that which we cannot see. It's believing against all visible evidence that what God has said is true. It's believing that the unseen is more real than the seen because the unseen exists in a reality apart from this world.

"And without faith it is impossible to please God," continues Hebrews 11:6, "because anyone who comes to him must believe that he exists and that he rewards those who earnestly seek him." Perhaps it's impossible to please God without faith because He Himself is invisible. To be sure of the God we cannot see, to hope for His promises to come to fruition in our lives, to be certain that He who has promised is faithful, and that He will also do it—that is faith. No wonder it's impossible to please God without faith.

In Hebrews 11, the hall of faith chapter, God lists the faith feats of people such as Enoch, Noah, Abraham, Isaac, and Moses—people who obeyed God because they believed God's promises concerning the future.

Hebrews 11:13–15 illustrates what was at the heart of their faith and the kind of faith God is looking for:

All these people were still living by faith when they died. They did not receive the things promised; they only saw them and welcomed them from a distance. And they admitted that they were aliens and strangers on earth. People who say such things show that they are looking for a country of their own. If they had been thinking of the country they had left, they would have had opportunity to return.

To help our children have faith-filled hearts, we need to do the following:

• Model a living faith for them. If we're afraid to trust God in everything and to put ourselves on the line to trust Him rather than fear and worry, how will our children learn to believe boldly in a God they cannot see?

• Open up God's Word to our children to help them hear the wonderful promises God has for them. Allow the Word of God to penetrate their hearts so they will believe God to fulfill what He has promised.

• Teach children that as believers in Jesus Christ, they are merely visiting this world; their real home is with God. Hebrews 12 paints a picture of us being surrounded by the people on the other side. Hebrews 12:1–2 says,

> Therefore, since we are surrounded by such a great cloud of witnesses, let us throw off everything that hinders and the sin that so easily entangles, and let us run with perseverance the race marked out for us. Let us fix our eyes on Jesus, the author and perfecter of our faith, who for the joy set before him endured the cross, scorning its shame, and sat down at the right hand of the throne of God.

Remember that according to Hebrews 11:13, the people in the hall of faith "admitted that they were aliens and strangers on earth." We are not home yet.

Faith has an incredible benefit for our relationship with the God we love. Scripture says in Hebrews 11:16 that because of their faith "God is not ashamed to be called their God, for he has prepared a city for them."

That is a worthy goal for our children to have—that God would be proud to be called their God! That happens by faith, and not just any faith. It's the kind of faith that helps our children see beyond the present to understand that there is a world beyond this one that is really the only one that matters. It's a faith that helps them invest in their heavenly accounts and live for that world, rather than spending their lives on things that in the end really don't matter.

Prayer for Today

I pray that out of the riches of Your glory You may strengthen my children with power through Your Spirit, so that Christ may dwell in their hearts through faith. And I pray that my children, being rooted and established in love, may have power to comprehend how wide and long and high and deep is Your love, and to know this love that surpasses knowledge—that they may be filled to the measure of all the fullness of God. Amen.

Based on Ephesians 3:16–19

Reflections

1. Why do you think lack of faith grieves God?
2. What difference would it make in your children's hearts to understand that they are "aliens and strangers" on Earth?
3. What difference does that understanding make for you?
4. How can you model this perspective for your children?

"'Have faith in God,' Jesus answered. 'I tell you the truth, if anyone says to this mountain, "Go, throw yourself into the sea," and does not doubt in his heart but believes that what he says will happen, it will be done for him. Therefore I tell you, whatever you ask for in prayer, believe that you have received it, and it will be yours.'"

—Mark 11:22–24

8

INCH BY INCH

"Folly is bound up in the heart of a child, but the rod of discipline will drive it far from him."
—PROVERBS 22:15

I don't even remember what his offense was, but when Grant was six, he had done something worthy of my telling him that he would not be able to go swimming with Abby and me that hot summer day.

Yet as I prepared to go to the pool, I felt sorry for him. How could I leave him? I caved in. "You can go with us, but you cannot get in the pool!" I told him emphatically.

After twenty minutes of Grant's sitting three feet from the pool while Abby and I played in the water, he could stand it no more. "Mom, can I just put my toes in the water?"

That face! How could I say no?

"Yes, but that's as far as you can go."

It was ten more minutes before Grant's calves were submerged in the water. I scolded him for taking advantage of the freedom I had given him. Back to dipping his toes.

Five minutes didn't go by before he tottered on the side of the pool and actually fell into the water—fully clothed!

I was furious! How could he have so grossly disrespected me when I was trying so hard to be nice to him?

We left immediately, and I fumed to Mike later. Wisely, he said, "Chris, you're going to win the battle but lose the war with Grant. I hate to think about what your relationship with him is going to be like when he's a teenager."

That cut right into my heart. I remember thinking how much I love Grant and long for us to have a healthy mother/son relationship. I needed to stop being his friend and start being firm if I wanted to nurture a healthy relationship.

When Grant was a bit older, I asked him to tell me what he thinks about when I delay disciplining him. He said, "I try to figure out what I can do to get out of trouble." He schemes. He inches closer to doing wrong. He takes a dive into more misbehavior.

Ecclesiastes 8:11 says, "When the sentence for a crime is not quickly carried out, the hearts of the people are filled with schemes to do wrong." This Scripture and the pool incident have been good motivating reminders for me to not delay the "sentence for a crime." Parents, it's better to discipline our children in a timely way than "wait till Mom or Dad gets home" or use any other delay tactic.

Delayed discipline is actually a training ground for our children's hearts to become defiled with scheming. Delayed discipline is a powerful tutor for our children—whether they're the offenders or the observers—to learn to be sneaky, manipulative, and/or deceptive. Delivering the appropriate discipline at the appropriate time helps keep our children's hearts pure.

Keeping their hearts pure is too important for us to do what feels right or nice or convenient. We need to do what may cause discomfort for a short time but will ultimately win each battle—and the war.

Prayer for Today

God, give me wisdom to be like You as I discipline my children. You discipline Your children because You love us—just as a father loves the child he delights in. God, You know how much I love my children. Help my children to neither despise nor resent the discipline You guide me to give them. Amen.

Based on Proverbs 3:11–12

Reflections

1. When it comes to disciplining your children, do you . . .
   • act too quickly,
   • act in the right amount of time, or
   • act later?
2. Explain your speed of action from the above question.
3. What changes do you need to make—if any—in your discipline timing in response to Ecclesiastes 8:11: "When the sentence for a crime is not quickly carried out, the hearts of the people are filled with schemes to do wrong"?

"Do not be quickly provoked in your spirit, for anger resides in the lap of fools."

—Ecclesiastes 7:9

9

HERE WE GO AGAIN

"Restore us to yourself, O LORD, that we may return;
renew our days as of old."
—LAMENTATIONS 5:21

Quit teasing your sister" became a familiar refrain on our last road trip.

"Stop taunting your brother."

"Quit making them mad!"

OK, who was getting mad now? Why can't we tell our children one time and be done with it? Why must we continually repeat many of the same charges to the same children all in the same day—and sometimes in the same sixty miles? Why won't children change?

Our children's genuine change—or repentance—is something we all long for as parents. It sure would make our job easier if once disciplined, our children forever repented from the offensive behavior. But, alas, it seems that we must deal with the same issues over and over.

I wish this were not the case, but the truth is, I guess they're just too much like us. First Kings 8:46 says that "there is no one who does not sin." We certainly know that's true of our kids, don't we?

But how many times in our own lives does God have to deal with us over and over—for the very same issues? Why don't we catch on faster? We continue to have the same sin that we must deal with—sometimes on a daily basis.

We sin against God, and God hates sin! Sin is against the very nature of God. It is an act of disobedience against a loving God who says, "Whoever has my commands and obeys them, he is the one who loves me" (John 14:21). Sin is an act of hatred toward God.

Because of that, there are spiritual consequences for sin. First Kings 8:46 says that sin angers God and causes the sinner to be taken captive by the Enemy. So, when our children sin or disobey in any way, they in essence become captive to the Enemy (or the devil). In effect, their sin makes it easier for the sin to be repeated—until they truly repent from the sin.

We parents need to understand this, because if we merely look at and deal with our children's behavior—and not their hearts—we haven't dealt with the spiritual reality of our children's sin or disobedience. Their behavior may stop, but if their hearts don't change, they're still captive to the sin. They must repent! But how do they get to the point of repentance?

We can't force repentance on our children. Our children are each so unique in their sensitivity and response to God's Spirit and our discipline.

When I was a child, all my parents had to do was scold me and I would start crying. My sister, however, even after a spanking, would turn around, square off with my parents, and say, "That didn't hurt!" More discipline would ensue. (I never understood why she wouldn't just soften her heart and cry. Then the discipline would be over!)

We can't force repentance, and to try to do so could become abusive. However, we can pray to the One who holds the reins of our children's hearts, and we can train our children to listen to His voice.

In 1 Kings 8:46, Solomon begins his prayer for his people with "When they sin against you—for there is no one who does not sin—and you become angry with them and give them over to the enemy, who takes them captive to his own land, far away or near. . ."

Solomon's prayer reveals that for Israel sin resulted in physical captivity to the nation's enemy. In the same way, our sin causes us to become captive to Satan's wiles. Yet we and our children don't have to reside in the Enemy's territory for long.

Solomon continues to pray,

> . . . and if they have a change of heart in the land where they are held captive, and repent and plead with you in the land of their conquerors and say, "We have sinned, we have done wrong, we have acted wickedly"; and if they turn back to you with all their heart and soul in the land of their enemies who took them captive . . . (1 Kings 8:47–48)

Solomon asks God to forgive them if they have a drastic change of heart that results in pleading or strong sorrow over the sin. Leviticus 26:41–42 implies that when their hearts are humbled, God will forgive. That's what Solomon is talking about. It takes abundant humility for children to admit that they're wrong, so we need to pray for the required humility for our children to repent.

Solomon continues praying in 1 Kings 8:49–51:

> Then from heaven, your dwelling place, hear their prayer and their plea, and uphold their cause. And forgive your people, who

have sinned against you; forgive all the offenses they have committed against you, and cause their conquerors to show them mercy; for they are your people and your inheritance, whom you brought out of Egypt, out of that iron-smelting furnace.

Let's look at these verses to help us better understand how to help our children move out of the Enemy's territory.

First, we must pray for our children. Yes, our children need to pray personally and confess their sins to God, but we also need to pray for the sins of our children and plead with God to forgive them and act on their behalf. I believe this is a starting point for our children to truly repent of their behavior and ultimately "own" their sin and admit it to God. (This was also the case in the prayers recorded in Nehemiah 1:5–11; Psalm 106:6; Daniel 9; and the promise given in Deuteronomy 30:1–3.)

Here are the truths we can pull from this passage about how to pray for our children. We need to:

1. **Pray that our children will have a change of heart.** Literally, that means "to turn back/to retreat." It's not enough for our children's behavior to change; we need to ask God to change their hearts so they retreat from the behavior.

2. **Ask God to help our children truly repent.** Literally, repent means "to breathe strongly; to be sorry." We can ask God to lead our children to the point of remorse so they are truly sorry for what they've done and confess their sin to Him.

3. **Ask God to restore our children, to forgive them, and to fight for them or "uphold their cause."** I can think of no greater thing that could happen after my children sin than to have the Creator of the universe restore, forgive, and fight for them.

4. Remind God that our children are His children. Solomon prayed, "for they are your people and your inheritance, whom you brought out of Egypt" (1 Kings 8:51). Our children are not our own; they are bought and owned by the blood of Jesus if they know Him as their Savior.

In Leviticus 26:42–45, God promises that He will remember His covenant with the Israelites because they are His people. Throughout the Old Testament, great leaders prayed for their people and appealed to God upon the basis of the existing relationship He had with His people. We can do the same.

Never give up! We need to continue to pray for our children and never give up on them. Even when the road is long, and the rest stops are few and far between, just keep praying!

Prayer for Today

God, help my children be truly repentant for their sin. May Your eyes be open to my plea and to the pleas of my children, and may You listen to us whenever we cry out to You. Amen.

Based on I Kings 8:52

Reflections

1. Consider each of your children. What are behaviors that each needs to repent of?
2. Write a prayer for each of your children, using I Kings 8:46–47 as your guide.
3. What does repentance look or sound like for each of your children?
4. Is there anything in your life that you need to repent of?

"Or do you show contempt for the riches of his kindness, tolerance and patience, not realizing that God's kindness leads you toward repentance?"

—Romans 2:4

10

FROM THE HEART

"Therefore judge nothing before the appointed time; wait till the Lord comes. He will bring to light what is hidden in darkness and will expose the motives of men's hearts. At that time each will receive his praise from God."
—I CORINTHIANS 4:5

After Mike and Tiffany Wagner returned home from church with their four children, their second oldest daughter, Rebekah, was in tears. Tiffany asked her what was wrong.

"She had a hard time at first telling me what was bothering her; she was very troubled," Tiffany remembers. "As we sat together and I kept encouraging her to open up, the story finally poured out."

Rebekah had been in a Sunday school class with the church's new children's minister. The children's minister had asked the children to tell her anything they didn't like about their Sunday school class. To motivate kids to open up, the children's minister offered a piece of candy for anyone who said something.

"Bekah is a bit shy," Tiffany explains, "but after seeing several children speak up and receive candy, she wanted a piece of candy also and decided to speak up. I asked her what she had said that she felt bad about. What was it she didn't like about the class?"

Rebekah said, "I said I didn't like the small groups during class." But then she broke out in tears and said this wasn't really true. What she felt so bad about was that she really liked all of her Sunday school class, but she just said something to get a piece of candy.

"The lie had tormented her so that she hadn't even eaten her candy," Tiffany says. "It was still in her coat pocket."

A week later at church Rebekah asked her parents if she could talk to the children's minister. She wanted to confess what she had done and give the candy back.

"Mike and I were both glad to see integrity from our seven-year-old and her willingness to confess and make things right," Tiffany says.

Rebekah was sensitive to the Holy Spirit and did the right thing. Yet her experience points to an alarming habit in motivating children—at church and at home.

At *Children's Ministry* magazine, we repeatedly request that people send us their great children's ministry ideas so we can publish them. I receive all kinds of ideas from people who minister to children. At least four or five times a year, I receive a "great idea" about "the Bible Buck Store" or something to that effect.

Perhaps your church has a similar system to motivate children. The premise is that when children do something worthy of reward, they get a Bible buck or token that they can redeem at the Bible Buck Store. Or they get a piece of candy or a prize as a reward.

Bring your Bible to church? Get a piece of candy.

Bring a friend or memorize a verse? Same reward.

Seems like a benign practice, but it's far from harmless. For one thing, this practice has its roots in secular behaviorism, not in the

Word of God. Behaviorism applied in the church assumes that if we give enough candy or prizes for the right things, children will begin to do the right things on their own when we remove the prizes.

B. F. Skinner's theory of behaviorism has influenced education for more than half a century. Skinner argued that all human and animal behaviors arise from the outside rather than from the inside of us. A behaviorist trains a dog to salivate when he rings a bell, thus changing the dog's behavior. Or he offers a sucker, and a kid recites a verse. The theory of behaviorism is not consistent with a biblical view of humans because it negates the role of the Holy Spirit in spiritual growth.

Why do we use behaviorism with our children? We want quick results. Why do we discount God's work in the hearts and minds of children? Although it seems we're getting the outward signs of spiritual growth, it's doubtful that we're causing inner change that results in long-term spiritual growth.

Ecclesiastes 7:7 says, "Extortion turns a wise man into a fool, and a bribe corrupts the heart." A bribe corrupts the heart! Why? Because it sullies pure motivation. Rather than focusing on doing good, a bribe makes us focus on a prize. It distracts us.

Some people argue that God is not opposed to rewards. In fact, they say, God has promised us Christians increased rewards in heaven commensurate to our obedience to Him. That's a point well taken, but can you imagine Jesus saying, "Follow Me . . . and I'll give you candy"? Or, "If you love Me . . . you'll get a new toy"? How about, "This is how all people will know that you're My disciples . . . if you have more Bible bucks than others"? Hard to imagine, isn't it?

Let's look at what the Bible says about rewards.

• **God Himself is our greatest reward.** The benefits, so to speak, of being a Christian come from a relationship with our

Creator. Genesis 15:1 says, "After this, the word of the LORD came to Abram in a vision: 'Do not be afraid, Abram. I am your shield, your very great reward.'"

• **Rewards come from obedience.** God doesn't reward our spiritual disciplines—although spiritual disciplines have their own reward. He rewards obedience, purity, and Christian love. Remember the story Jesus told in Matthew 25:34–46. Jesus said God will reward those who feed the hungry, give a drink to the thirsty, visit the prisoners, and clothe the naked. Jesus doesn't say that rewards will be passed out for those who memorize a verse.

• **Rewards are for things done in secret.** Every time we give children a reward, we may rob them of an eternal reward. Matthew 6:1–4 says,

> Be careful not to do your "acts of righteousness" before men, to be seen by them. If you do, you will have no reward from your Father in heaven. So when you give to the needy, do not announce it with trumpets, as the hypocrites do in the synagogues and on the streets, to be honored by men. I tell you the truth, they have received their reward in full. But when you give to the needy, do not let your left hand know what your right hand is doing, so that your giving may be in secret. Then your Father, who sees what is done in secret, will reward you.

• **Rewards are for more than just coming to church.** We tend to reward the rudiments of children's spiritual disciplines, while Jesus says that rewards are for so much more. In Matthew 10:41–42 Jesus says,

> Anyone who receives a prophet because he is a prophet will receive a prophet's reward, and anyone who receives a righteous man because he is a righteous man will receive a righteous man's

reward. And if anyone gives even a cup of cold water to one of these little ones because he is my disciple, I tell you the truth, he will certainly not lose his reward.

What are proper motives then? If we are to avoid the trinket economy of motivation, how can we motivate our children?

The best motive is love for God. Jesus said in John 14:15, "If you love me, you will obey what I command." Love is the proper motive for obedience. Yet we often demand obedience without the love relationship. We need to introduce children to a loving God, help them nurture a love relationship with Him, and guide them into actions that are pleasing to Him. Until our children's love relationship with God is in place, as Christian parents we can and should expect obedience to God's standards and to household rules, but meanwhile we are modeling our own obedience that flows out of our love for God.

When Grant was five, I asked him what he would do if talking about Jesus would get him into trouble at school. He said, "I'd talk anyway." "Why?" I asked. "Because Jesus loves me best" was the pure response of a small child who had experienced our Savior's love—the right enticement for obedience.

Seminary professor James Rosscup, who has studied the biblical view of rewards, asserts that in Scripture, "Jesus insists that the motive is the heart of what pleases God. Just doing an act in itself may not be faithfulness. Reward is for why you do what you do."

Prayer for Today

God, I pray that my children would serve You wholeheartedly. Thank You, God, that You reward everyone for whatever he or she has done for You. Please keep my children's hearts set on You rather than the reward. Amen.

Based on Ephesians 6:7–8

Reflections

1. What is your philosophy about the use of rewards in motivating your children?
2. Do you agree or disagree with the philosophy presented in this chapter? Explain.
3. If dessert is offered for kids to eat their spinach, what might promised rewards communicate about the thing we're trying to entice them to do? (This is the "spinach principle.")
4. How can you help your children fall so in love with God that their love for God is their greatest motivation?

"Behold, I am coming soon! My reward is with me, and I will give to everyone according to what he has done. I am the Alpha and the Omega, the First and the Last, the Beginning and the End."

—Revelation 22:12–13

11

HEAVENLY TREASURE

"Jesus answered, 'If you want to be perfect, go, sell your
possessions and give to the poor, and you will have
treasure in heaven. Then come, follow me.'"
—MATTHEW 19:21

Weeds are the weirdest thing to me. They can sprout up any-where and everywhere. Weeds' express purpose is to seek out any non-weed living thing and choke it to death.

Some of the weeds in our yard are beautiful—even with flow-ers on them. Their beauty is deceptive, though. One weed has blooms that resemble a morning glory flower. For a while, it lulled me into thinking it wasn't a weed. I allowed it to stay in my garden until it threatened the life of my plants. It was a real chore to remove.

Another weed is something I had never seen until I moved to Colorado. It's also deceptive because it looks like a lovely ivy. Yet, left unchecked, it climbs "good" plants and chokes them out. It's called bindweed.

We're all familiar with dandelions. As a child, these funny little plants delighted me. I would pluck the fuzzy round dandelions and blow like crazy to spread them all over our yard. I didn't know until I was much older that I was seeding my dad's yard with nasty little weeds.

And worst are the prickly weeds that almost seem to bite back when pulled. Every now and then, I overconfidently reach down without gloves to pluck one of these humdingers out of the ground; the next day, I live with the memory of those little prickly edges in my hands.

No matter what kind of weed grows in my yard, I've learned that they have to go. And I've discovered that there's a fine art to killing weeds. I first started my adventure of weed-pulling with dandelions and my bare hands. That didn't work; I could not get the entire root out of the ground.

Then we bought a special weed-pulling instrument that required good timing as I had to step on a lever while I inserted its teeth into the ground, then put all my weight on it to pull up the dandelion by its root. When successful, the entire root would come out intact—and it would leave quite a divot on the ground. Yet I was amazed at how such a small weed could have such a long root—sometimes as long as eighteen inches!

In Mark 4:18–19, Jesus talks about a different kind of weed that needs to be plucked out before it chokes the life of the Word in our children's hearts. In explaining the parable about the sower and the seeds, Jesus says, "Still others, like seed sown among thorns, hear the word; but the worries of this life, the deceitfulness of wealth and the desires for other things come in and choke the word, making it unfruitful."

The worries of this life, the deceitfulness of wealth, and the desires for other things come in and choke out the Word. Materialism. The thirst for more. More stuff. More things. More money. More toys. When we fall into materialism, our appetite for stuff is never satisfied.

Scripture says that materialism is a sure guarantee for the Word of God being choked out of our children's hearts. By guiding our children's hearts away from materialism, we'll help Mark 4:20 be true of our children: "Others, like seed sown on good soil, hear the word, accept it, and produce a crop—thirty, sixty or even a hundred times what was sown."

God is not calling all of us to take a vow of poverty. But He is asking us to put money and material possessions in their proper place in our hearts. Actually, it's not so much about having things as it is about what we set our hearts on. Psalm 62:10 says, "Though your riches increase, do not set your heart on them."

Since the heart is the center of everything in our life, God is saying to not make riches the center of our lives. How can we practically keep material possessions in their proper perspective?

Matthew 6:19–21 gives us the answer to that question. Jesus says, "Do not store up for yourselves treasures on earth, where moth and rust destroy, and where thieves break in and steal. But store up for yourselves treasures in heaven, where moth and rust do not destroy, and where thieves do not break in and steal. For where your treasure is, there your heart will be also."

How can our children store up treasure in heaven? What we treasure, we give our money, time, and mental energy to. Each time our children tithe or give to the church, a mission organization, or anyone in need, they are storing up treasure in heaven. Each time they serve others, they're storing up treasure in heaven.

When they are storing up treasure on earth, their "treasure" becomes the focus of their lives and stands in the way of their being available to God. I remember once when I was single and someone was encouraging me to go to China to teach English as a second language. The primary obstacle that came to my mind was a living thing; I couldn't imagine leaving my dog. As it turns out, God did not call me to go to China, but that was a wake-up call about where my treasure really was.

God calls us to serve Him and not money. Jesus says in Matthew 6:24, "No one can serve two masters. Either he will hate the one and love the other, or he will be devoted to the one and despise the other. You cannot serve both God and Money."

How can we tell if our children are serving money? God, in His goodness, has given us the answer to that question in the next verses. In Matthew 6:25–34, Jesus tells His followers not to worry about such passing needs as the life and the body, or the supplies to take care of it. Worrying about food is useless: "Look at the birds of the air; they do not sow or reap or store away in barns, and yet your heavenly Father feeds them. Are you not much more valuable than they?" (v. 26). Worrying about clothing is also needless, because God knows that need as well:

> And why do you worry about clothes? See how the lilies of the field grow. They do not labor or spin. Yet I tell you that not even Solomon in all his splendor was dressed like one of these. If that is how God clothes the grass of the field, which is here today and tomorrow is thrown into the fire, will he not much more clothe you, O you of little faith? So do not worry, saying, "What shall we eat?" or "What shall we drink?" or "What shall we wear?" For the pagans run after all these things, and your heavenly Father knows that you need them. But seek first his kingdom and his righteousness, and all these things will be given to you as well. Therefore do not worry about tomorrow, for tomorrow will worry about itself. Each day has enough trouble of its own. (vv. 28–34)

An additional litmus test for our children's heart focus is worry. If they are worried about earthly things, then they have made them the center of their lives. We need to model for our children and encourage them to have complete trust in God's ability to provide all needs. If worry about things is choking our children's hearts, we need to help them skillfully pull those weeds up so the entire worry root is eradicated.

Prayer for Today

God, I pray that You would protect my children from setting their hearts on what they eat and drink and play with. I pray that, rather than worrying about such things, they would trust You to provide for them. I know that You know that they need these things. I pray that they would seek Your kingdom first. As they do that, thank You that You will take care of all of their needs. Help them to give sacrificially to those in need. Lord, help them to invest their treasures in eternity so that their hearts will be there also. Amen.

Based on Luke 12:29–34

Reflections

1. What would be the most difficult thing(s) you might have to give up for the kingdom of God? Could that thing(s) be standing in your way of serving God fully?
2. Are there any needs you are currently worried about? If so, give those to God and watch Him faithfully provide.
3. If you had a statement for your earthly account of treasures and your heavenly account of treasures, which would have the larger balance? Explain.

Family Exercise

Try this exercise with your children. Have two people stand side by side in the center of a large room or outside in your yard. Have your children look at both people at all times. Then have both people walk in opposite directions until they can go no farther. Afterward, ask your children how easy or difficult it was to keep their eyes on both people at the same time. Then read Matthew 6:24 and discuss how your family can keep from serving money and instead stay focused on God only.

"Two things I ask of you, O LORD; do not refuse me before I die: keep falsehood and lies far from me; give me neither poverty nor riches, but give me only my daily bread. Otherwise, I may have too much and disown you and say, 'Who is the LORD?' Or I may become poor and steal, and so dishonor the name of my God."

—Proverbs 30:7–9

12

PURIFY YOUR HEART

"Surely God is good to Israel, to those who are pure in heart."
—PSALM 73:1

My husband's grandmother married young to an affluent man. Never before had she experienced the niceties that her husband's wealth afforded.

One thing she was particularly enamored with was her new silver tea set. Yet, when it began to tarnish from its bright silver appearance to a dull darkness, she was dismayed. *Maybe it isn't so fancy after all,* she thought, as she threw it in the trash.

Years later, she realized that the only thing the silver had needed was to be polished to retain its previous luster. By then it was too late.

And so it is with our children's hearts. For us to expect that our children will always have pure hearts is naive. The world pushes in on them; and, like our silver, their hearts tarnish. If we over-react to the tarnish we see on their hearts, they will feel thrown out and will languish under our unrealistic expectations of them.

While we guide our children, we need to continually pray against the things that can tarnish their hearts. Psalm 73 tells us the things to guard our children's hearts from. This psalm clearly helps us understand what a pure heart is by itemizing what it is not.

Those who are not pure of heart are arrogant and conceited. They rave about how great they are and so appear to be foolish. Scripture says that "the evil conceits of their minds know no limits" (Psalm 73:7). They are verbally and physically abusive. They unrighteously oppress others; they are your kid's worst nightmare at school—bullies. Their hearts are calloused and filled with sin.

Of course, your child doesn't fit the above description because your child is a Christian. Right?

I hope it's right. Yet, in my work with children in the church, it's not always true. In fact, it is sadly true that many churched kids are the most exclusive and unkind at school—even to the very kids who attend church with them. We parents need to ask God for a clear objectivity to know our children, to know their weaknesses and strengths. If impurities such as the above are present in our children's hearts, we need to deal with those first.

Your child is probably not one of the bullies at school, but he or she may be one of the bullied children. Your child is more than likely one of the children who watches the ungodly children around him and wonders why they seem to prosper. Why is it they get all the friends? They never get in trouble. Why is it that "they are free from the burdens common to man; they are not plagued by human ills" (Psalm 73:5)?

It was this line of thinking that caused the writer of Psalm 73 to "almost slip." As the psalmist looked at the wicked people around him, his heart was filled with envy. Envy is even stronger than jealousy in that envy desires to deprive the envied person of what he has. Envying evil things brings them closer to our hearts. If left unchecked, envy becomes arrogance, pride, violence, and oppression. Soon, envy can cause your child's pure heart to be filled with sin and become calloused, unable to respond to the promptings of the Holy Spirit.

Psalm 73:15–28 gives the solution to envying the wicked and almost slipping. Thankfully, the psalmist realized what was happening to him. So he told God, "I was senseless and ignorant; I was a brute beast before you" (v. 22). A few key things pulled the psalmist out of the miry place of envy. First of all, he felt an obligation to his brothers and sisters in the faith. He wrote, "I would have betrayed your children" (v. 15).

For us as parents, this is a powerful tool to help children walk uprightly. Remind them that they are an example for those around them. Help them see that if they fail to be upright, they may lead others astray.

Second, the psalmist wrote that it was oppressive to him to try to understand why the wicked person prospers until "I entered the sanctuary of God; then I understood their final destiny" (v. 17). The psalmist prayed. He cried out to God for understanding. We can encourage our children to do the same.

The psalmist realized that everything is not as it seems. Children can look at the kids with the cool clothes, the great looks, the amazing gifts, and think that is what's most important. If our children don't move beyond the values of this worldly kingdom to develop heavenly kingdom values, they'll cycle again through envy and the pursuit of the things that will defile their hearts.

The psalmist understood that what really matters is seeing things from an eternal perspective. What will really matter when this world passes and what remains is the next life? The psalmist "understood their final destiny"; he understood that there will be a judgment day and everyone will be repaid. We must model for our children that we're living for the next world rather than just this one. And we must challenge them to do the same.

Third, the psalmist sought comfort in the presence of God. He wrote, "Whom have I in heaven but thee? and there is none upon earth that I desire beside thee. My flesh and my heart faileth: but God is the strength of my heart, and my portion for ever" (Psalm 73:25–26 KJV).

This brings us to a simple three-step plan to use when we see our children struggling with envy and not understanding why good is not always rewarded, but bad sometimes seems to be rewarded.

1. Be near God. We must encourage our children to draw near to God. James 4:7–8 tells us to "Submit yourselves, then, to God. Resist the devil, and he will flee from you. Come near to God and he will come near to you. Wash your hands, you sinners, and purify your hearts, you double-minded."

The very act of drawing near to God purifies our children's hearts. This can be done by spending time praying and reading God's Word together, by encouraging our children to have personal devotions with God, and by encouraging them to pray about everything all day long.

2. Make God your refuge. We need to encourage our children to cry out to God for understanding. Prayer is not a formulaic, formal undertaking. It is the conversation of our deepest heart cries with a loving God.

3. Tell of all His works. The psalmist closes with "I will tell of all your deeds" (Psalm 73:28). Encourage your children to tell others—in your family, at church, or elsewhere—the amazing things that God is doing in their lives, teaching them, or saying to them. The very act of celebrating God's works not only glorifies God, but it also helps reinforce the reality of God in our children's lives and thereby keeps their feet from slipping.

Prayer for Today

God, help my children not to fret over or be envious of people who do wrong. Help them to understand that these people will wither like the grass. Instead, help my children to trust You and to do good so they may know Your security and safety. Lord, help them to delight in You—and then to be surprised by joy as You give them the desires of their hearts. Lord, as they commit their ways to You, I know You will act on their behalf. You will make their righteousness shine brightly. May they learn to wait patiently for You and to hope in You forever. Amen.

Based on Psalm 37:1–9

Reflections

1. Would you say that you have realistic or unrealistic expectations for the purity of your children's hearts?
2. Who could you talk to at each child's school and Sunday school class to get an objective view of your child?
3. What is it that most tempts your children to be envious?

Family Exercise

Dramatically model for your children what it means to cry out to God. In their best desperate voices, tell your children to loudly cry, "God, help me!" Have them do this with you.

They may laugh at your temporary strangeness, but when the time comes for them to cry out to God, they'll understand the emotional honesty they can have with God. Don't hold back.

"A heart at peace gives life to the body, but envy rots the bones."

—Proverbs 14:30

13

FRUIT OF
THE MOUTH

"Set a guard over my mouth, O LORD;
keep watch over the door of my lips."
—PSALM 141:3

M om, what does 'do-do' mean?" Grant asked me one day in the car when he was four.

"It's another word for 'potty,'" I answered.

The next day in the car again: "Mom, what does 'do-do' mean?"

"Grant, why? Where have you heard that?"

"At church, we sang a song to God and said 'do-do-do-do'!" Oops!

I guess he couldn't accept that he was singing my definition of the word to God. Singing "potty-potty" to God just didn't jibe with his four-year-old theology. Nor mine, for that matter!

OK, I'm guilty as charged—assuming something without asking enough questions to really know what my child was saying. But who among us hasn't been guilty of the same mistake at one time or another?

Once we take the time to discover what our children are talking about, we'll get a glimpse into their hearts. In Luke 6:43–45, Jesus says,

> No good tree bears bad fruit, nor does a bad tree bear good fruit. Each tree is recognized by its own fruit. People do not pick figs from thornbushes, or grapes from briers. The good man brings good things out of the good stored up in his heart, and the evil man brings evil things out of the evil stored up in his heart. For out of the overflow of his heart his mouth speaks.

A child's speech is the barometer of his heart. What does he talk about? What do his words reveal about his attitudes? What is it that he is not saying when you talk with him?

Truthfully, the easiest way to know our children's hearts is to simply talk with them. Mike and I have a practice of "dating" our children. We take each of them out for individual time every now and then. It can be as simple as going shopping and getting a soft drink or as complex as playing laser tag with a meal afterward. As we talk to each of our children, we better discover what's in his or her heart.

Apart from better understanding our children's hearts, our goal is that they have and continue to develop pure speech. If it is true that the fruit of our children's mouths reveals their hearts, we want to inspire them to have pure hearts that result in pure speech.

Here are a few guidelines from Scripture:

• Encourage children to be an example for others in how they speak.

"Don't let anyone look down on you because you are young, but set an example for the believers in speech, in life, in love, in faith and in purity." (1 Timothy 4:12)

• **Encourage children to understand that their speech is a large part of their testimony for Christ.**

"In everything set them an example by doing what is good. In your teaching show integrity, seriousness and soundness of speech that cannot be condemned, so that those who oppose you may be ashamed because they have nothing bad to say about us." (Titus 2:7–8)

• **Encourage children to speak words that help others.**

"Do not let any unwholesome talk come out of your mouths, but only what is helpful for building others up according to their needs, that it may benefit those who listen." (Ephesians 4:29)

• **If your children use words carelessly, encourage them to say less instead of more.**

"When words are many, sin is not absent, but he who holds his tongue is wise. The tongue of the righteous is choice silver, but the heart of the wicked is of little value." (Proverbs 10:19–20)

As we talk to our children, seek to understand them better, and encourage them to pursue pure speech, we'll be singing a new song —just as my son did when true understanding arrived on the scene.

Prayer for Today

God, Your Word says that we all stumble in many ways and especially in what we say. Lord, since no man can tame the tongue by himself, I pray that You will help my children to tame their tongues. Help them to honor You with pure hearts that result in pure speech. Amen.

Based on James 3:2, 8

Reflections

1. How pure is your speech? Rate yourself on a scale of 1 to 10 (with 1 being "get out the soap mouthwash" and 10 being "where's my halo?").

2. Rate each of your children with the above scale. What does the "fruit" of your children's mouths tell you about their hearts?
3. Which of the four scriptural guidelines listed in this chapter could you focus on today with your children?

Family Exercise

Try this exercise with your family. Have everyone in your family hold their tongue with his or her forefinger and thumb. Have each person talk for thirty seconds in this way. Everyone gets a turn. Afterward, ask how easy or difficult it was to understand one another. Then read aloud James 3:2–8, and discuss ways other than "holding our tongues" that we can seek to control our tongues. (If you really want to gross out your kids and make this memorable, serve beef tongue for dinner!)

"He who loves a pure heart and whose speech is gracious will have the king for his friend."

—*Proverbs 22:11*

14

CUT TO
THE HEART

*"But I tell you the truth: It is for your good that I am going away.
Unless I go away, the Counselor will not come to you; but if I go, I will
send him to you. When he comes, he will convict the world of guilt in
regard to sin and righteousness and judgment."*

—JOHN 16:7–8

Our youngest child, Reed, has the most sensitive spirit of any
child I've ever known. Sometimes even before I notice that he's
done something offensive, he will come to me and say, "Mom, I'm
sorry. Will you please forgive me?"

"What are you sorry for?" I'll ask.

"I'm sorry that I didn't respect you and listen to you."

Wow! I wish I were that sensitive to the Holy Spirit's conviction in my life.

Lamentations 1:20–21 uses these words to describe conviction:
distressed, in torment within, and *groaning.* The writer of Lamentations
says that "in my heart I am disturbed, for I have been most rebel-
lious." I long for that kind of grieving over sin in my life.

Sometimes I've had that ultrasensitivity to the conviction of
the Holy Spirit, and then other times I've allowed my heart to

become hardened to the Holy Spirit's conviction. In those times, it takes God a little longer to get my attention. Because of the delay, I find that my discomfort in being convicted of sin can last a bit longer as well—until I confess my sin and get right with God.

If I were to project my parental feelings on God, I suppose that I would see Him as being frustrated with my slowness to acknowledge my sin and repent. However, Romans 2:4 says, "Or do you show contempt for the riches of his kindness, tolerance and patience, not realizing that God's kindness leads you toward repentance?"

God's patient kindness leads us to repentance. God sees the end, and rather than just wanting to get things over with (which I am often guilty of in my parenting), God wants the right outcome—a genuine change of heart.

As parents, we need to allow our children to experience the discomfort of conviction. In fact, we need to avoid the "quick-fix-apology syndrome" we often use; and, instead, give God time to work on our children's hearts.

See if this sounds familiar: One of your children offends another, and rather than dealing with the root issues such as selfishness or pride, the quick answer is to put a Band-Aid on the situation by saying, "Now, tell your sister that you're sorry." On the surface, everything gets better, but deep inside, there is still "death" as the writer of Proverbs 18:21 would put it.

What can we do then?

For one thing, if our children are Christians, we can be sure that the Holy Spirit is committed to convicting them of sin. John 16:7–8 says, "But I tell you the truth: It is for your good that I am going away. Unless I go away, the Counselor will not come to you; but if I go, I will send him to you. When he comes, he will convict the world of guilt in regard to sin and righteousness and judgment."

If our children do not yet believe in Jesus Christ, the Holy

Spirit will convict of sin and wrongdoing. If our children are believers in the Lord Jesus Christ, the Holy Spirit will also guide their hearts into righteousness. Our important job is to teach our children to listen to the Holy Spirit—and to respond in obedience.

So, of course, the most important requirement for our children to love God with all their heart is that they need to know Christ as their Savior. Until then, we can guide our children with biblical principles—and even their consciences can guide them—but true heart-change in which they'll love God with all their heart is not possible. It is only by the Holy Spirit's work from within that godly conviction can work on our children's hearts.

The second thing we can do is to avoid rushing an apology from our children. It is better to send a child to his room with the instructions to think about what he has done—and even to pray about it—than to have children insincerely apologize. Avoid sending your child to his room with the admonition, "When you're ready to say you're sorry, you can come out." That's a sure guarantee for short-circuited heart work. While your child is in his room, pray that God would speak to him.

After ample time in his room, check back with the child to see what God has done in his heart. Avoid pat questions that have "right" answers, such as, "So are you sorry for what you did? Are you ready to come out? Do you understand what you did wrong?" Instead, ask open-ended questions such as, "So what did you think about? How do you feel about what happened? What do you think God would want you to do now?"

And what if your child says, "I don't know" or "Nothing" (which will probably be the case at times)? Explain to your child the spiritual consequences of a lack of repentance, such as broken relationships with people or God. Pray with your child. Then say something like "I believe God is still dealing with you. I want you to tell me what God shows you later." Remember: You can't control

God's work in hearts or children's responses to God. Yet, by following these steps, you create a training ground for children to learn to listen to God.

What is the result of genuine conviction? In Acts 2, Peter preached in the power of the Holy Spirit a convincing sermon about who Christ is. Peter finished his sermon with "Therefore let all Israel be assured of this: God has made this Jesus, whom you crucified, both Lord and Christ" (v. 36). Scripture says that when the unbelievers heard this, they were "cut to the heart." The righteous response to genuine conviction is a desire to do the right thing—not just get rid of discomfort. "Brothers, what shall we do?" they asked (v. 37).

The unrighteous response to conviction is to do nothing at all. Yet the severe consequence of not responding to conviction is a hardened heart. Hebrews 3:12 says, "See to it, brothers, that none of you has a sinful, unbelieving heart that turns away from the living God."

The solution? Hebrews 3:13 says to "encourage one another daily, as long as it is called Today, so that none of you may be hardened by sin's deceitfulness."

Getting away with sin leads to a hardened heart. We must, as parents, be diligent to watch over our children's behavior yet not rush to quick "solutions." By encouraging them to listen to God's voice and respond appropriately to the Holy Spirit's conviction, we help shape their hearts to be wholeheartedly God's.

Prayer for Today

God, I pray that You will keep my children's hearts open to You. I pray that because of who You are, they will know You and long to submit to You. God, I cry out for my children and ask that You never give them over to a stubborn heart. Please keep their heart pliable in Your hands. Amen.

Based on Psalm 81:11–12

Reflections

1. What does it feel like when God convicts you of sin?
2. Describe a time that you responded righteously to conviction of sin and a time that you responded unrighteously to conviction of sin. Which had the more positive outcome? Explain.
3. For each of your children, what are specific evidences of conviction of sin in his or her heart?
4. Why is it tempting for parents to rush an apology from their child rather than to allow time for God to work in the child's heart? Think of a time that you rushed an apology from your child. What was the outcome?

"Tell the king of Judah, who sent you to inquire of the LORD, 'This is what the LORD, the God of Israel, says concerning the words you heard: Because your heart was responsive and you humbled yourself before God when you heard what he spoke against this place and its people, and because you humbled yourself before me and tore your robes and wept in my presence, I have heard you, declares the LORD.'"

—2 Chronicles 34:26–27

15

MAKE A
JOYFUL SOUND

"My heart is steadfast, O God, my heart is steadfast; I will sing and make music. Awake, my soul! Awake, harp and lyre! I will awaken the dawn. I will praise you, O Lord, among the nations; I will sing of you among the peoples. For great is your love, reaching to the heavens; your faithfulness reaches to the skies. Be exalted, O God, above the heavens; let your glory be over all the earth."
—PSALM 57:7–11

I had just graduated from seminary with a Master of Divinity—the study of theology. The study of God.

For three years, I had devoted my life to studying all the ins and outs of God, His church, His world, His Word. I had committed my life to Christ only three years before that, and I had lived for nothing since then but to know, love, and follow this very real God who had reached into my life and pursued me with His love.

After graduating from seminary, I moved home for the summer to raise my support to do mission work on a college campus in preparation to go overseas in two years as a foreign missionary. I longed to devote my entire life to serve God wherever He wanted, doing whatever He asked me to do.

While in seminary, my roommates and I hadn't had a television, so my exposure to things such as MTV had been limited.

My younger brother, however, had a steady diet of television and MTV.

Thinking I should become more culturally literate to be able to reach college students, I watched the music videos with him every now and then. I figured that since I was going to be working with college students, I should understand their world better. I learned a big lesson about the difference between observing and experiencing the world—or being in the world but not of it.

My parents live in a very small town. One of my daily highlights was walking to the river, where a ribbon of red cuts through lush green pastures and is backdropped by clear blue skies. One day while taking my walk, I was startled by this thought: *How can I even believe there is a God?*

"What? Who?"

I was stunned—and rattled. Here I was raising my support to be a missionary. How could such a thought have entered my mind?

I will never forget how clearly God impressed me that watching the music videos on MTV had subtly planted seeds of doubt in my heart and mind. Now, don't think that I was watching blatantly God-bashing videos. (This was almost twenty years ago, so they were milder back then.) To the contrary, I was watching what I considered to be decent videos; the other kind would have had me scrambling for the remote control to switch them off.

Because of this experience and others, I am thoroughly convinced that music has a powerful effect on our hearts. As parents, we have a wonderful opportunity to use music to minister to our children and to infiltrate their hearts. We also have the responsibility of guiding our children's music decisions.

Ephesians 5:18 cautions us: "Do not get drunk on wine, which leads to debauchery. Instead, be filled with the Spirit." We're to "speak to one another with psalms, hymns and spiritual songs. Sing and make music in your heart to the Lord, always giving thanks to God the Father for everything, in the name of our Lord Jesus Christ" (vv. 19–20).

David says in Psalm 108:1 that his "heart is steadfast," and therefore he "will sing and make music with all [his] soul." Psalm 138:1 stresses that praise comes from a whole heart. David says, "I will praise you, O LORD, with all my heart."

Our hearts must get in position to worship God. That's why it is so important to involve our children in worship at church and in our homes. Sometimes when our family is on the cranky side, I like to turn on worship or classical music that plays softly in the background. It's amazing to watch how it soothes our spirits. I am sure the process is very similar to what David did for Saul in 1 Samuel 16:23: "Whenever the spirit from God came upon Saul, David would take his harp and play. Then relief would come to Saul; he would feel better, and the evil spirit would leave him."

I am not saying that my family has an evil spirit, but sometimes we need calmer music to give us relief and make us feel better. Music soothes our spirits.

How can you know which music is appropriate for your children? How can you discern which music will cause your children to sing and make music in their hearts to the Lord?

Try these filters for testing music.

With your child, read the lyrics and put them through the Philippians 4:8 filter: "Finally, brothers, whatever is true, whatever is noble, whatever is right, whatever is pure, whatever is lovely, whatever is admirable—if anything is excellent or praiseworthy—think about such things." If the lyrics can pass these tests, they are OK for shaping your child's heart.

Then listen to the music together. Ask God for discernment about the beat and the rhythm. I was shocked one day when I brought home a contemporary Christian artist's CD to review for the magazine I edit. As I played it, Grant walked through and commented that it sounded like "devil music." God will give you and your children discernment to know which music is appropriate for you.

Finally, music isn't just something for the here and now. Heaven is filled with music. Zephaniah 3:17 says, "The LORD your God is with you, he is mighty to save. He will take great delight in you, he will quiet you with his love, he will rejoice over you with singing." Encourage your children's hearts with the image of their Creator delighting in them and singing over them.

Prayer for Today

God, I pray that You would let the peace of Christ rule in my children's hearts. I pray that You will fill their hearts with peace and thankfulness. I pray that You would help them to let the Word of Christ dwell in them and give them wisdom. Fill their hearts with psalms and songs of gratitude to You. Amen.

Based on Colossians 3:15–16

Reflections

1. How has music affected your heart?
2. How has music affected your children's hearts?
3. Based on the filters in this chapter, are there any changes you need to make in the music your family is exposed to?
4. How and when can you add soothing music to your home? Or, if you have music or other noise in your home too much of the time, how can you add silence?

"Sing to the LORD a new song, for he has done marvelous things; his right hand and his holy arm have worked salvation for him."

—Psalm 98:1

16

ROAD TO REPENTANCE

"This is what the Sovereign LORD, the Holy One of Israel,
says: 'In repentance and rest is your salvation, in quietness
and trust is your strength, but you would have none of it.'"
—ISAIAH 30:15

Early this year, Grant broke his arm at school. His slip on the ice slammed his body onto the cement. Emergency surgery, hospitalization, one plate, four bolts, and one red cast later, his arm was finally unsheathed. Naked and unprotected, his arm was wide open for reinjury, and I feared for his safety. Through therapy and time, his arm has gotten stronger, but it's still tender.

That's what made this exchange I'm going to tell you about even more difficult. At bedtime (when reserves are low for children and parents), Reed was on Grant's pillow. So Grant said something harsh and jerked the pillow out from under Reed.

Reed, of course, lashed out at Grant and kicked his vulnerable arm. As Grant cradled his wounded appendage in his other hand, he looked at me and asked, "Aren't you going to do something?"

Normally, I probably would have dealt rather severely with a child who lashes out physically. That's one area where we have very little patience—no physical contact, no matter how mad you are.

But this had been one of those days. The boys had been bickering off and on all day and just didn't seem to enjoy each other at all. There are seven years between Grant and Reed, and that in itself creates a challenge. However, Mike and I are committed to helping our children grow up to be friends—starting now.

"No, I'm not going to do anything," I said, even surprising myself. "If you are not going to work on having a healthy relationship, that is what's going to happen. You two are going to keep hurting each other until you decide to become friends."

I thought about my decision afterward and halfway saw the wisdom in it, because it was all about natural consequences. How would they ever understand the severity of their sin toward each other if I always rushed in to fix it? I want them to understand that their sin toward each other not only has momentary consequences, but, if not dealt with, it also has severe consequences for their lifetime relationship as brothers—and ultimately as men of God. And, yet, inside I hoped that I'd made the right decision.

The next day I saw the fruit of my actions. Grant and Reed played outside together for a long time as they built a fort. And they played happily! I could see that they were reconciling on their level, working to get along as brothers. The fruit of repentance in their life was actual change on this particular day.

Jeremiah 31:18–21 has helped me because it gives a clear picture of what's involved in leading our children to repentance for their sins—their outright disobedience or rebellion. In verse 18, God says, "I have surely heard Ephraim's moaning: 'You disciplined me like an unruly calf, and I have been disciplined. Restore me, and I will return, because you are the LORD my God.'"

The word *discipline* here means literally to "chastise with blows" and figuratively to "chastise with words." The word *discipline* also involves correction, teaching, reproof, binding, reforming, and making sore. So for Ephraim's offense, there was a clear consequence or punishment. For us as parents, sometimes we need to allow a natural consequence, and other times we need to mete out a punishment that makes kids feel sore or uncomfortable.

Once disciplined, though, God's goal with Ephraim was restoration. Ephraim says, "Restore me, and I will return." And the same is true for our children; we want them to be restored. In the King James Version, this verse says "turn thou me," which paints the picture of a bull unaccustomed to the yoke being brought under submission of the yoke.

Take a look at the next verses to see how this is accomplished. Jeremiah 31:19 says, "After I strayed, I repented; after I came to understand, I beat my breast. I was ashamed and humiliated because I bore the disgrace of my youth." *Repent* in verse 19 means to "breathe strongly." Or we can think of it as a heavy sigh. The grieving over the sin (beating the breast) came after he understood.

OK, I have a confession. Sometimes when Mike lectures our children, I can't wait for it to be over. I often think, *Why would they ever disobey, since they know they'll have to hear the lecture?* God used these verses to show me how wrong I am. Discipline is not just about punishment; it's also about instruction so our children can understand the shame or the consequences of their sin.

All discipline is in the context of a loving relationship. Ephraim in Jeremiah 31:18 affirms that God is "the LORD my God." That's a strong affirmation of relationship. And then in verse 20, God says that Ephraim is "my dear son, the child in whom I delight." The verse continues: "Though I often speak against him, I still remember him. Therefore my heart yearns for him; I have great compassion for him."

God affirms the relationship by saying "my dear son." The word *son* comes from the word that means "builder." Here, it means "builder of the family name." God is expressing how connected He is to Ephraim. And when He says "I still remember him," He is saying that He "marks him so as to remember him" in an ongoing relationship. And God says that He has "compassion" or sympathy for Ephraim.

Any discipline that we give our children—whether it's punishment or instruction—needs to be loving as it flows from a relationship that has been established over time. We also have to have a vision for who our children are—they are the builders of our family name.

Prayer for Today

God, I ask You to lead my children to grieve over their sin—not a worldly repentance that causes death, but a godly sorrow that leads to repentance. Amen.

Based on 2 Corinthians 7:9–10

Reflections

1. What is the difference between natural consequences and punishment?
2. How can you communicate your love for your children even while disciplining them?
3. Why is restoration critical to disciplining your children?
4. What—if anything—bothers you about the way your spouse disciplines your children? If you and your spouse disagree, talk about the differences to discover the reasons for your different methods.

"Repent, then, and turn to God, so that your sins may be wiped out, that times of refreshing may come from the Lord."

—Acts 3:19

17

AN UNDIVIDED HEART

"Then you will call upon me and come and pray to me,
and I will listen to you. You will seek me and find me
when you seek me with all your heart."
—JEREMIAH 29:12–13

Our daughter, Abby, started playing soccer a couple of years ago. The first season, she had a coach who led her team to an undefeated season. Her coach helped the girls understand the fundamentals of the game, but that was about all. She didn't yell at them, and she wanted them to have fun as they played. We figured that was the best it could get.

The next season, we registered Abby with different coaches. We didn't know them, but the time and place they practiced was more convenient for us.

Let me tell you, Dean and Laura Miller, Abby's new coaches, are in a league by themselves. They showed up the first day with soccer equipment we had never seen before. They ran the girls through assorted drills to keep things interesting each time they practiced. They were organized and on top of the entire aspect of coaching a soccer team.

Not only did Dean and Laura coach the team, but their two girls Sidney and Cheyenne were on the team too. I watched with interest as Dean and Laura delighted in their daughters' antics and in their growth as soccer players.

After two more seasons with only one loss for our team, Dean and Laura asked if Abby could be on a special team that would compete in a local tournament. Abby loves soccer, so we said yes.

Again, the Millers were on top of everything. They gave us schedules, directions, and more to keep us in the know. They called us to line up a meeting time for Abby and the other players to tie-dye socks and T-shirts for their uniform. They provided pizza for a soccer party afterward.

We found out along the way that not only did Dean and Laura do all this for their younger daughters, but they also coached their oldest daughter, Samantha, in a competitive league and in the special tournament Abby was invited to join. Two teams at once! And next year, it will be three!

This family seems to eat, live, and breathe soccer. I think they are a great example of wholeheartedness. They've invested their time and energy consistently in what they feel is beneficial to their girls. They do it with an amazingly good attitude and have been able to pass on their love for soccer to the children. They haven't merely talked about soccer or watched it on TV or even just shown up at weekly soccer games. No, they have immersed themselves wholeheartedly as a family into the game.

We have a lot to learn from Dean and Laura about wholeheartedness. If we want our children to be wholehearted for God, we must be wholehearted for God. We can't have a weekend-only religion; our faith must consume us throughout every day of our lives. Evidence of our wholeheartedness for God will be in how we spend our time and money, what we talk about, and what we intentionally involve our children in.

What does it mean for our children to be wholehearted for God? In 1 Chronicles 28:9, the term "wholehearted devotion" means the same thing as "perfect heart." That's what we're talking about when we talk about wholeheartedness; it's having a heart that's perfect, undivided, toward God.

God's wonderful promise for such a perfect heart toward Him is that we will seek Him and find Him. Deuteronomy 4:29 says, "But if from there you seek the LORD your God, you will find him if you look for him with all your heart and with all your soul." What a promise! God is not a God who hides from us and is ambivalent toward us knowing Him. God longs for us to seek Him with fervor, and He will reveal Himself to us and our children.

Other promises for wholehearted devotion to God involve God's blessings for our lives. In Deuteronomy 30:2–3, God says, "And when you and your children return to the LORD your God and obey him with all your heart and with all your soul according to everything I command you today, then the LORD your God will restore your fortunes and have compassion on you and gather you again from all the nations where he scattered you."

What does wholehearted devotion to God look like? Deuteronomy 26:16–17 stresses that someone with a whole heart toward God will obey God. This Scripture says, "The LORD your God commands you this day to follow these decrees and laws; carefully observe them with all your heart and with all your soul. You have declared this day that the LORD is your God and that you will walk in his ways, that you will keep his decrees, commands and laws, and that you will obey him."

"Impossible!" you say. Not at all! Deuteronomy 30:11 says, "Now what I am commanding you today is not too difficult for you or beyond your reach."

It can be done! Our children can love God with all their heart. The key thing for us to do is to create an environment that does not allow their hearts to be enticed away to something else, as

Samuel talks about in 1 Samuel 12:20–21: "'Do not be afraid,'
Samuel replied. 'You have done all this evil; yet do not turn away
from the LORD, but serve the LORD with all your heart. Do not
turn away after useless idols. They can do you no good, nor can
they rescue you, because they are useless.'"

Over and over in Scripture, God stresses staying away from
idols. In Deuteronomy 11:16, He says to "be careful, or you will
be enticed to turn away and worship other gods and bow down
to them."

The key to helping our children love God with all their heart
is in the first two words of Deuteronomy 11:16—be careful!

"Be careful" literally means to take heed to yourself or to put
a hedge about yourself. A hedge in the Old Testament was built
of stones—not like the green hedges we think about today. It was
used to fence in, to cover over, or to hedge in. It was a boundary
of protection—to keep out harmful elements.

In Ecclesiastes 10:8, we find that there is danger if one goes
past the boundary hedge: "Whoever digs a pit may fall into it;
whoever breaks through a wall may be bitten by a snake."

A hedge was a common boundary in Jesus' day. Jesus mentions
it in a parable in Mark 12:1: "A man planted a vineyard. He put a
wall around it, dug a pit for the winepress and built a watchtower.
Then he rented the vineyard to some farmers and went away on
a journey."

And in the Old Testament, adulterous Gomer had left her husband and children to commit adultery. God used Gomer as an
illustration for Israel, who insisted on "prostituting" herself with
other gods. God hedged Israel in so she could not go back to her
lover but would instead return to Him. In this case, God used the
hedge to create restraint. In Hosea 2:5–7, God says,

Their mother has been unfaithful and has conceived them in disgrace. She said, "I will go after my lovers, who give me my food

and my water, my wool and my linen, my oil and my drink." Therefore I will block her path with thornbushes; I will wall her in so that she cannot find her way. She will chase after her lovers but not catch them; she will look for them but not find them. Then she will say, "I will go back to my husband as at first, for then I was better off than now."

So what can we learn from all these hedges in Scripture? For our children to love God with all their heart and be obedient to all He has revealed, we need to set boundaries for them. We must watch over what our children are exposed to and what they are giving their hearts to.

Years ago, I knew of a wealthy Christian father who each year bought a new car for his family. He noticed one year in particular that one of his sons was overly interested in the entire car venture. The son focused on what kind of car it would be, even to the point of idolatry.

Very wisely, this father created a boundary over his son's affection by not buying a car for the family that year. Instead, the father bought a car for a missionary family that depended on others for their financial support. By doing this, the father helped break the hold the new car had on his son's affections.

I experienced something similar recently. I had joined a weight-loss organization to shed some pounds. After five months in the program, God revealed to me that I was spending entirely too much time and energy on the topic of dieting. It wasn't the diet that was the problem; it was my obsession with the program details, weight-loss Websites and magazines, and conversations about dieting that God wanted me to release. I quit the organization and stopped my obsession.

I remember standing in an airport bookstore during this time and staring at the magazines. (I'm a magazine editor, so I love to read magazines!) I stood two feet away from the racks and scanned the covers. I knew inside that I couldn't handle the slimmer thighs, flatter abs magazines.

"You're not letting me buy a magazine, are you?" I prayed to God. It was as though He had built a hedge around me to keep me from idolizing dieting in my life.

Since that time, I've rejoined the organization and followed its program. As I said, it wasn't the dieting that was the problem; it was my focus. I've learned to keep dieting in its proper place.

That's exactly what we need to do for our children—we need to help them keep things in their proper place in their hearts. We need to pray and ask God to give us wisdom and discernment in this area. Then we need to help our children by establishing boundaries around them. Perhaps the boundary is less time in front of the television or video games. It may be limited time with a certain friend. Or even a curtailment on spending habits.

Whatever it is, the best gift we can give our children in this area is to establish boundaries at all times and to rein in those boundaries when necessary.

Prayer for Today

God, I pray that You will turn my children's hearts to You to walk in all Your ways and to keep the commands, decrees, and regulations You have given us. And may these words of mine, which I have prayed before You, be near to You day and night, that You may uphold my cause and the cause of my children. May those we know see through us that the Lord is God and that there is no other. I pray that my children's hearts would be fully committed to You, to live by Your decrees and obey Your commands. Amen.

Based on 1 Kings 8:58–61

Reflections

1. Think of the most wholehearted person you know. What makes this person wholehearted?
2. What percentage of your heart would you say belongs to God?

3. What percentage of your children's hearts would you say belongs to God?

Family Exercise

To help your children understand being wholehearted, make a paper heart. With your family, discuss the things that can take a person's heart away from God. Each time something is mentioned, tear a piece off the heart. Destroy one or two of the pieces entirely. Then try to put the heart back together, and discuss with your family the importance of keeping their hearts whole for God.

"But be very careful to keep the commandment and the law that Moses the servant of the LORD gave you: to love the LORD your God, to walk in all his ways, to obey his commands, to hold fast to him and to serve him with all your heart and all your soul."

—Joshua 22:5

18

AMAZING GRACE

*"Blessed is the man who always fears the LORD, but he
who hardens his heart falls into trouble."*
—PROVERBS 28:14

If you ever question whether God can soften your child's hard heart, be encouraged by Albert Cheng's story.

Albert was a Buddhist living in Cambodia in 1972 when wars raged around him. Albert remembers that the "smell of blood and human carnage was horrible" at that time. Albert cried out, "Where is God? Is there a God?" The only one Albert could ask was Buddha, but Buddha was silent.

In 1975, Albert was imprisoned in a concentration camp where people were tortured, beaten, and starved day and night. Again, Albert cried out for God. And there seemed to be no answer.

Each time Albert cried out to God for help and felt there was no answer, his heart hardened a little bit more. He distrusted everyone around him. Once, he says, he saw a white crane fly over the camp, and he longed for the freedom the bird had, but he believed he would never be free again.

Finally, Albert and fourteen other young men escaped the concentration camp. They lived in the jungle for three months by eating cobras, wild rats, and bugs; they drank sap from the vines. Traveling only at night, they finally made it to the Thailand border.

A field of land mines, poison-dipped bamboo sticks, and thousands of bullets stood between them and freedom. They forged ahead, though, because of their thirst for freedom. Only two of the fifteen survived.

Albert says, "I knelt down, looked at the moon, and thanked God" when he made it safely, but he still wondered, "Who is God?"

Albert first learned of Jesus Christ in the Thai refugee camp when Christian missionaries showed him a film about Jesus. Although he could tell that Jesus was a nice man, he couldn't understand any of the language. He also couldn't understand why Jesus was put to death.

A Christian organization sponsored Albert's coming to the United States in the Dallas area. Although God seemed distant to Albert, He always seemed to give Albert jobs in churches.

Albert still sought God in the Buddhist ways. He says, "I went in the church sanctuary to meditate and turned my back on the cross. I sought God very hard. I went to temple and fasted, but there was no hope. I joined with the Buddhists and wore their black robe and chanted with them."

Albert felt that the more he sacrificed in the Buddhist ways, the more he saw the people at Canyon Creek Presbyterian Church smiling. They loved one another and had peace, things Albert longed for.

In 1996, Albert returned to Cambodia. He grieved the deaths of his sister and brother, who were brutally killed by the Communists. Albert says, "I wanted to join a guerrilla group, take a bazooka or AK-47, and get revenge."

Albert came back to Canyon Creek with a spiritual war raging inside him. His heart was hardened even more by hatred and revenge. The God he had been crying out to had never answered him, Albert thought, yet he still longed to know if there was a real God.

Mary Hodge, the Christian education director at Canyon Creek, was one of God's answers to Albert's prayers. Mary offered to read the Bible with Albert. As they met regularly, the Word of God came alive for him. Yet because of his hard heart, he continued to follow the Buddhist ways.

God's miraculous power to melt hearts met Albert in his sleep in 1997. Albert dreamed that he saw a huge cross. As he looked at the cross, lightning struck him in the forehead.

About his dream, he remembers, "The sound of beautiful music came from inside of me, and I passed out. Then a shining form like a human being sat next to me. I couldn't look; it was too bright. The figure disappeared and the most wonderful peace came over me. I felt like I was floating off the bed. The sound of music grew louder and stronger."

Albert awoke, smiling, and he couldn't go back to sleep.

The next morning, Albert hurried to find Pam Miller, the Discovery School music teacher at Canyon Creek. He didn't recognize the beautiful music and wanted to know what it was. He hummed the music he had heard in his dream. "Albert, are you crazy?" Pam asked incredulously. "That's 'Amazing Grace'!"

Albert ran to the sanctuary, opened a hymnal, and read the words to the song. He wept as God's peace swept over him and softened his heart.

He was baptized and professed Jesus Christ as his Lord and Savior on February 22, 1998. Since then, he has grown in his walk with the Lord through discipleship and study of the Word.

When I met Albert this year, his faith in Christ shone brightly as he shared his story with me. He now co-teaches a class for children at Canyon Creek so they too can know and love the living God.

Albert says now, "Perhaps one day God will send me back to Cambodia—not with an AK-47 or a bazooka, but with a guitar and the Word of God!"

Albert's heart was hard because he had not accepted Jesus Christ as his Savior. Even so, the living God was watching over him, protecting him, and wooing him to Himself. Albert did not understand that for a long time. Albert's story is a wonderful example of the persistence of God to continue to work in our lives and draw us to Himself, despite our hard hearts.

As was the case with Albert, a hardened heart keeps our children from experiencing the presence and the power of God in their lives. What can we do to help them keep their hearts soft toward God?

Scripture is quite clear that hardened hearts result from the rejection of God's revealed truth to us and blatant unbelief. In Zechariah 7:11–13, God says of Israel,

> But they refused to pay attention; stubbornly they turned their backs and stopped up their ears. They made their hearts as hard as flint and would not listen to the law or to the words that the LORD Almighty had sent by his Spirit through the earlier prophets. So the LORD Almighty was very angry. "When I called, they did not listen; so when they called, I would not listen," says the LORD Almighty.

Our children harden their hearts by not listening to God's Word. And the consequence of that is that God will become deaf to their pleas. We don't want that to happen. So what does it mean to listen to God's Word? The obvious answer is obeying what

God's Word says, but a more subtle agent that hardens hearts is simply not getting it. Missing the point. Not understanding fully. It is listening to biblical accounts and walking away entertained but not affected by the real truth revealed.

As I studied the Word for this chapter, my heart was stirred because I realized that it is so easy for us to not get it—especially when we study the Word of God so much that the stories seem mundane. We are at risk of becoming immune to truth's impact because of familiarity.

That's a risk for our children as well, especially if as Christian parents we have surrounded them with quality Christian education at home and church. The stories they've heard from infancy may be just that—stories.

In the Gospels, the disciples didn't get it even when they watched Jesus feed two different multitudes. In the gospel of Mark, Jesus challenges His disciples not once, but twice, to look beyond the miracles to get the point so their hearts will not be hardened.

After the feeding of the five thousand, Jesus went to His disciples by walking on the water. His disciples saw Jesus and immediately reacted with fear. They thought He was a ghost and cried out. Jesus said, "Take courage! It is I. Don't be afraid" (Mark 6:50).

After Jesus climbed into the boat with them, the Bible says that the disciples "were completely amazed (v. 51)." The word *amazed* in the original language means that they were out of their wits, astounded, and filled with wonder. Their amazement, in this case, was not one of honor or praise. It was shock! Mark 6:52 explains why their amazement was not a good thing by saying they were amazed "for they had not understood about the loaves; their hearts were hardened."

They missed it! They did not get that Jesus is the living God, the Creator of everything—and therefore Master of the physical elements. He can multiply food, walk on water.... He can do anything. If the disciples had realized this, they wouldn't have been shocked. They may have been in awe but not beside themselves with amazement.

Again, after the feeding of the four thousand, Jesus confronted His disciples at sea for not getting it. Jesus warned His disciples to "watch out for the yeast of the Pharisees" (Mark 8:15). The disciples immediately began to discuss that Jesus must be mad at them for not bringing bread along. In Mark 8:17–21, the account unfolds:

> Aware of their discussion, Jesus asked them: "Why are you talking about having no bread? Do you still not see or understand? Are your hearts hardened? Do you have eyes but fail to see, and ears but fail to hear? And don't you remember? When I broke the five loaves for the five thousand, how many basketfuls of pieces did you pick up?"
>
> "Twelve," they replied.
>
> "And when I broke the seven loaves for the four thousand, how many basketfuls of pieces did you pick up?"
>
> They answered, "Seven."
>
> He said to them, "Do you still not understand?"

We need to be careful that our children are infected with the truths of the Word of God, rather than being inoculated by it. What can we do, as parents, to help our children "get it"?

• **Ask God for help.** Like the father who brought his son to Jesus to be healed, we need to pray for God to help us and our children with our unbelief. In Mark 9:23–24, Jesus said to the father, "Everything is possible for him who believes." The father exclaimed, "I do believe; help me overcome my unbelief!"

• **Teach biblical accounts, not stories.** We need to avoid teaching the truths of the Bible as mere stories. Rather, they are accounts of God's encounters with His people that reveal truth about who He is. We need to ask God to reveal His truth to us before we read the Bible with our children. Then after each reading, we can discuss with our children what the account reveals about who God is.

• **Turn to God.** We need to encourage our children to turn to God because He can take care of them. For example, in Psalm 53:5, God says, "There they were, overwhelmed with dread, where there was nothing to dread." If we truly understand who God is and what He can do, we have nothing to dread ever. All of our fears, anxieties, and dreaded things can be met with the awareness that God is able to take care of anything we face.

Prayer for Today

God, thank You that there is no longer a veil covering our minds to make them dull and our hearts hard. Rather, in Christ, You have removed that veil. I pray for my children that with unveiled faces, they will reflect Your glory. Thank You that as You reveal Yourself to them, they are being transformed into Your likeness with ever-increasing glory, which comes from Your Spirit. Amen.

Based on 2 Corinthians 3:12–18

Reflections

1. Are you aware of any unbelief in your heart? If so, confess it to God and ask Him to help your unbelief.
2. Is there anything that you believe God is not able to take care of in your life? If so, what is there that has been revealed in Scripture about God that would contradict your unbelief?
3. How have you ensured that Your children are learning the accounts of the Bible? How can you encourage them to see the God who is revealed in each of these accounts?

Family Exercise

Make a list of all the things that are revealed about God in Bible accounts. With your children, add to the list each time you read the Bible. Whenever any of you faces a faith challenge, refer to the list to see how God is able to take care of it.

"So I tell you this, and insist on it in the Lord, that you must no longer live as the Gentiles do, in the futility of their thinking. They are darkened in their understanding and separated from the life of God because of the ignorance that is in them due to the hardening of their hearts."

—Ephesians 4:17–18

19

CELEBRATE!

"Sing, O Daughter of Zion; shout aloud, O Israel! Be glad and rejoice
with all your heart, O Daughter of Jerusalem! The LORD has taken
away your punishment, he has turned back your enemy. The LORD,
the King of Israel, is with you; never again will you fear any harm."
—ZEPHANIAH 3:14–15

Every year at Easter my pastor, Kent Hummel, tells us about his non-Christian neighbor's take on Easter since it's a big day of rejoicing for the church.

"Hey! It's almost time for your Super Bowl, isn't it?" he asks Kent.

"Yeah, I guess it is," Kent says with a laugh. One year, our church even printed invitations that looked like Super Bowl tickets for our Easter service. I figure they were a big hit with men!

The year the Denver Broncos won their second Super Bowl, I happened to be at a children's ministry conference in Denver. The day of the parade, several of us went up to the top of the hotel to watch the sea of people. I stayed for a little while, but then I made the mistake of leaving the hotel to get coffee at a Starbucks store.

The roar was deafening as the Denver Broncos drove by. Thousands of people lined the streets, rejoicing at the Broncos' victory. I decided that a winning sports event such as a Super Bowl championship is one of the best examples of what rejoicing looks like.

I have to admit that I've seen more of what looks like rejoicing at sporting events than I have in churches. And I wonder how our children will ever know what rejoicing looks or sounds like in our somber services.

What exactly causes rejoicing? And why does God tell His people to "rejoice with all your heart" in Zephaniah 3:14?

Rejoicing is a celebration in our hearts. In 1 Chronicles 16:10, we're told to "glory in his holy name; let the hearts of those who seek the LORD rejoice." The word *glory* means to make a show, to boast, and to be clamorous. That, to me, sounds like the reaction at a sports event. But, seriously, how many of us are ever willing to make a show as we celebrate God? It seems everything has to be restrained and controlled. It would do us good to act as though we're at a parade once in a while when we're in church.

What causes such rejoicing? The following verses shed light on that.

First Chronicles 16:11–14 says, "Look to the LORD and his strength; seek his face always. Remember the wonders he has done, his miracles, and the judgments he pronounced, O descendants of Israel his servant, O sons of Jacob, his chosen ones. He is the LORD our God; his judgments are in all the earth."

In the above passage, rejoicing is clearly a response to God's face, strength, wonders, miracles, and judgments. Rejoicing is a response to who God is and what He has done in our lives and in the world.

The Greek word for rejoicing is *chairo,* which means joy. This word is directly related to *charis,* the Greek word for grace. The connection between these two words sheds light on an exciting aspect of rejoicing.

Charis (grace) is God's unmerited favor toward and acceptance of us. There is absolutely nothing we—or anyone else—can do to deserve God's grace. It is given simply because of who God is. Grace emanates from a gracious, loving God who is holy in everything He does.

Chairo (rejoicing), then, is a direct result of God's grace. Rejoicing is a response to God's wonders, miracles, judgments, and strength. Rejoicing because of God's grace helps us to say, with the psalmist who wrote Psalm 16:2, "Apart from you I have no good thing."

The psalmist was able to say that because he was content with God's provision in his life. He saw God's grace in everything. Take a look at Psalm 16:5–6: "LORD, you have assigned me my portion and my cup; you have made my lot secure. The boundary lines have fallen for me in pleasant places; surely I have a delightful inheritance."

His portion, his cup, his lot, his boundaries, his future—the psalmist rejoices in God's grace in all these pleasant places.

Paul says in Philippians 3:1 that rejoicing is a safeguard for us, and in Philippians 4:4 that we are to rejoice always. Paul says that rejoicing is a safeguard for us because if our minds are fixed on all the amazing things that God has done, and if we're aware of and even actively looking for God's grace in our lives, then our minds are Spirit-controlled. Romans 8:5–6 says, "Those who live according to the sinful nature have their minds set on what that nature desires; but those who live in accordance with the Spirit have their minds set on what the Spirit desires. The mind of sinful man is death, but the mind controlled by the Spirit is life and peace."

When we think about the importance for our children's hearts of rejoicing, it will be tempting to have them perform the act of rejoicing. "You need to be more excited about God," we may say. Or, "Act like you really love God when you worship." This focus on the external is the wrong response. We must focus instead on rejoicing being a "grace response."

We need to help our children identify God and His grace in their lives. As we do that with them, their natural response will be rejoicing in their heart.

Prayer for Today

God, I praise You because You hear my prayers. I pray that You will be my children's strength and shield. I pray that their hearts will trust in You and that You will help them. As a result, God, I know that their hearts will leap for joy and they will give thanks to You. Lord, be the strength of my children—their fortress of salvation. Save my children and bless them. Be their Shepherd and carry them forever. Amen.

Based on Psalm 28:6–9

Reflections

1. Describe a time when you saw or experienced genuine rejoicing.
2. Describe a time when you saw each of your children experience genuine rejoicing.
3. With your family, list the wonders and miracles you can celebrate from the Bible.
4. With your family, list the wonders and miracles you have seen God perform in your lives.

Family Exercise

Gather your family together and surprise each family member with a small gift. When asked what the gift is for, explain that no one did anything to deserve the gift; you just wanted to give them something. Use this experience to talk with your children about how God's grace is like that—no one can do anything to deserve it.

This week, send your children on a grace scavenger hunt. Encourage them to see who can find the most evidences of God's grace in their lives. (Invisible things such as oxygen count!)

"All the days of the oppressed are wretched, but the cheerful heart has a continual feast."

—*Proverbs 15:15*

20

GOURMET GRATITUDE

"Give thanks to the LORD, for he is good;
his love endures forever."
—PSALM 118:1

I'm no gourmet chef. And I'm no short-order cook, either. OK, I'm not a very good cook at all.

To be a good cook, you have to measure things, follow recipes, and have the right ingredients on hand. I'm a dump-it-in, fly-by-the-seat-of-my-pants, substitute-it-if-it's-the-same-color kind of cook.

And the comments from my family reflect my approach to meal preparation. I'm expedient, not artistic, when it comes to cooking. As long as my family is getting the basic food groups and the meal isn't burned, they need to eat it.

But every now and then, a not-so-gracious childlike comment slips out from one of my children. Like the night I nuked some kind of low-fat chile relleno casserole that I'd made a couple of months before and frozen. Grant looked at it, poked around in it, and then politely said, "If I was stranded on a desert island and this was the only food, I'd eat it."

Thanks, Son!

Or the time I made a chicken, black bean, and mango dish on rice. This was so healthy! I placed individual bowls in front of each person and asked Grant to pray. He dutifully bowed his head and stared at his bowl. The only thing he could come up with was "I wish we'd gone to Chuck E. Cheese!"

My inability to wow my family with delicious meals has been a sore spot for me, but I'm finally realizing it's OK that I'm not the greatest cook. After all, my family can always get good cooking at Grandma's!

Our need to protect our children from discomfort, pain, or suffering (in other words, my cooking), and to give them the very best of everything, may actually rob our children of learning to give thanks when things are less than perfect.

Don't be discouraged if you feel that life is not perfect for your children. As they learn to give thanks in the midst of imperfection, they will learn to love God with all their heart. And their character will have many more opportunities to develop through imperfection rather than perfection.

What are our children to be grateful for? Everything! They are to give thanks because God has been so good to them in providing for them and taking care of them. Acts 14:17 says, "Yet he has not left himself without testimony: He has shown kindness by giving you rain from heaven and crops in their seasons; he provides you with plenty of food and fills your hearts with joy."

Other Scriptures related to thanksgiving also give insight into what we and our children are to thank God for.

• **The gift of joy**—"You turned my wailing into dancing; you removed my sackcloth and clothed me with joy, that my heart may sing to you and not be silent. O LORD my God, I will give you thanks forever." (Psalm 30:11–12)

• **For who He is; not just what He has done**—"Praise the LORD. Give thanks to the LORD, for he is good; his love endures forever. Who can proclaim the mighty acts of the LORD or fully declare his praise?" (Psalm 106:1–2)

• **For what He has done**—"Let them give thanks to the LORD for his unfailing love and his wonderful deeds for men, for he satisfies the thirsty and fills the hungry with good things." (Psalm 107:8–9)

• **For the Word of God**—"At midnight I rise to give you thanks for your righteous laws." (Psalm 119:62)

• **For food**—"And he directed the people to sit down on the grass. Taking the five loaves and the two fish and looking up to heaven, he gave thanks and broke the loaves." (Matthew 14:19)

• **For victory**—"But thanks be to God! He gives us the victory through our Lord Jesus Christ." (1 Corinthians 15:57)

• **For answered prayer**—"I will give you thanks, for you answered me; you have become my salvation." (Psalm 118:21)

• **For everything**—"Give thanks in all circumstances, for this is God's will for you in Christ Jesus." (1 Thessalonians 5:18)

What are some practical ways to help our children give thanks to God continually? Try these ideas.

• **Gratitude journal**—Suggest that each child keep a personal journal where he or she writes prayers of thanksgiving to God. Or have a family journal and periodically write things that each person is grateful for.

• **Modeling**—Give your children a good example of your own thanksgiving to God by praying before each meal and praying aloud with your children at the end of the day.

• **A, B, Cs**—One game our family likes to play on the way to Grandma and Grandpa's house for Thanksgiving is to go through the alphabet and think of all the things we're thankful for that begin with each letter.

Whatever you do, embrace the life that God has given you and your children by thanking Him every day for taking care of you.

Prayer for Today

God, thank You so much for my wonderful children. I pray that You would give them the spirit of wisdom and revelation so that they may know You better. As a result, I pray that their hearts may be enlightened so they may know the hope to which You have called them, the riches of Your glorious inheritance, and Your incomparably great power for those of us who believe. As a result, God, I pray that their hearts will overflow with gratitude to You. Amen.

Based on Ephesians 1:16–19

Reflections

1. What—if anything—in your life have you been ungrateful for? Explain.
2. No one has a perfect life. Take time to think of the positive things about any imperfect situation your family is facing.
3. Which things in your children's attitudes might be evidence of a lack of gratitude (for example, whining, resentment, or comparing)?

"Give thanks to the LORD, for he is good; his love endures forever."

—1 Chronicles 16:34

21

TRUST
AND OBEY

*"Does the LORD delight in burnt offerings and sacrifices as
much as in obeying the voice of the LORD? To obey is better
than sacrifice, and to heed is better than the fat of rams."*
—I SAMUEL 15:22

For more than a year, God had quietly but persistently whispered in my ear to commit to the children's ministry at our church. I wasn't really thrilled with the proposition because of how busy my life was at the time. At any rate, I told Mike that I felt that God was calling me to give some of my time to our children's ministry.

Mike reminded me of all the things I already had on my plate, but he said that if God was calling me to do it, it was fine with him.

I didn't hear the last part of what he said. And it didn't take much convincing for me to use the busyness excuse again. I met with our Christian education committee and gave them a laundry list of ways I could serve. Wisely, they sensed my reluctance and asked me to do only one thing. I breathed a sigh of relief and led the monthly teacher training.

One year later, God gripped my heart strongly while I attended a conference, and He gave me a vision of what He wanted to do in our church's children's ministry. My mind was a blur of exciting possibilities and all my excuses: I'm too busy; our family time is already limited; I don't want to hurt the current leaders' feelings; I don't have my personal life together; and so on and so forth.

God revealed to me my brokenness at the same time that He was revealing His awesomeness. Each excuse melted away as God seemed to be saying, "It's not about you; it's about what I want to do in and through you."

When I returned from the conference, I called the deacon in charge of our Christian education committee. "I have to talk to you!" I said in my message. I called the next day and left the same message. This time he heard my wholehearted desire to serve.

I discussed the vision with him and the Christian education committee, and then with our newly formed Dream Team—whom God had also prepared to jump onto this new vision. The people I'd worried about offending breathed a huge sigh of relief. They admitted that for a year, God had been leading them to step back from leadership.

We revamped our children's ministry, and we experienced tremendous joy and fruit in our children's and volunteers' lives. As I experienced the wonder of being a colaborer with God, I was a different person with a new life-giving purpose that blessed our church and my family.

One morning, after making this commitment, I realized that my spirit was singing "Yes, Lord!" over and over. I stopped and understood the sweet rewards of saying yes to God. It truly was like a well of water springing up in me.

That's the amazing thing about obedience—it's nothing but joy on the other side! That's what our children need to hear as well—that obeying God results in pure joy and a sense of blessing.

I am not saying that all of life will be perfect when we obey, and our children need to know that. Yet God does promise to give us blessings when we are faithful to obey Him. In Deuteronomy 11:13–15, God says,

> So if you faithfully obey the commands I am giving you today—to love the LORD your God and to serve him with all your heart and with all your soul—then I will send rain on your land in its season, both autumn and spring rains, so that you may gather in your grain, new wine and oil. I will provide grass in the fields for your cattle, and you will eat and be satisfied.

Over and over, God promises to pour out blessings to those who obey Him. We need to encourage our children to obey God with all their heart and all their soul out of reverence for their God. The benefit of that obedience is abundant blessing.

Is one of the blessings personal righteousness, as Deuteronomy 6:24–25 suggests? These verses say, "The LORD commanded us to obey all these decrees and to fear the LORD our God, so that we might always prosper and be kept alive, as is the case today. And if we are careful to obey all this law before the LORD our God, as he has commanded us, that will be our righteousness."

To some degree in terms of our daily practice of living the Christian life, it is our righteousness. But as far as our righteousness before God, that comes only from our faith in Jesus Christ. First Corinthians 1:30 says, "It is because of him that you are in Christ Jesus, who has become for us wisdom from God—that is, our righteousness, holiness and redemption."

As we model obedience for our children and as we encourage them to also obey God, we need to be careful to communicate the actual role of obedience; it is not to gain God's favor.

Abby and Reed love to play games such as "don't step on the cracks of the sidewalk" or "you can only step on the brown tiles."

If I happen to step on the wrong things, they tell me, fire will shoot up out of the earth.

I wonder if sometimes that's what we communicate to our children—a complex set of rules to follow that have severe consequences if they are broken. Instead, we need to help them see that obedience is a response of love to a God who has given us unconditional favor through the sacrificial death of His Son. God's grace covers all our failures, but what joy there is when we are saying yes to the God we love!

Prayer for Today

God, I pray that my children will be men and women after Your own heart and that they will do everything You want them to do. Amen.

From Acts 13:22

Reflections

1. Think of a time you said yes to God and experienced great joy. Describe that time.
2. If God is calling you to obey in an area where you've been reluctant, what excuses are you using? Ask God to erase those excuses.

Family Exercise

A great way to teach your children about complete obedience is to play a game such as Mother, May I? or Simon Says. After the game, use these discussion questions:

- How were the consequences for breaking the rules similar to or different from the consequence of disobeying God?
- How were the rewards of following the rules similar to or different from the rewards for obeying God?

"This has been my practice: I obey your precepts. You are my portion, O LORD; I have promised to obey your words."

—Psalm 119:56–57

22

CAST YOUR BREAD

"Give, and it will be given to you. A good measure, pressed down, shaken together and running over, will be poured into your lap. For with the measure you use, it will be measured to you."
—LUKE 6:38

When Loren Cunningham was a young boy, he arrived at the church where his father was pastor to find a brand-new red Jeep parked inside the church building. His father explained to the surprised congregation that a missionary in Dahomey (now Benin), West Africa, needed a Jeep for transportation to preach the gospel in a village called Natitingou.

Along with the rest of the congregation, Loren gave sacrificially to the cause. He even gave two months of income from his newspaper route. Not only was Loren's heart prompted to give generously, but he also began to pray for the missionary, for the country, and for the Natitingou. The church was successful at paying for the Jeep and had it shipped overseas to the missionary.

Years later, after Loren had grown up, he founded a dynamic mission organization called Youth With a Mission (YWAM). So he was asked to visit Natitingou as a speaker.

Loren got to ride in the very Jeep that his church had bought for the missionary. In the University of the Nations publication *Online*, Loren remembers, "It was about ready for Jeep heaven at that time, but it thrilled me to ride in it and to preach in Natitingou."

One day, Loren received a call from the secretary of President Mathieu Kerekou of Benin. The president wanted Loren to teach him from the Word of God on how to be a leader according to the Bible.

Loren went to the country and taught the president. In their conversations, Loren told the president about the Jeep. He remembers telling the president, "Where you put your treasure, there will your heart be also. God used that Jeep to plant a love in my heart for your nation."

The president exclaimed, "I was born and raised in Natitingou!"

The president had been in Natitingou when the Jeep arrived. The president asked Loren to teach his cabinet and tell that story to them also.

God used a simple gift from a young man to affect a nation and its leader. God also used the simple gift to shape a young man's heart—the heart of a man who would found a mission organization that has affected the world and young people's lives for years.

It is not an option to teach our children to be generous givers. It is our responsibility.

In helping them to give generously, follow these six basics of giving.

• Give generously from your heart—not grudgingly.

"So I thought it necessary to urge the brothers to visit you in advance and finish the arrangements for the generous gift you had promised. Then it will be ready as a generous gift, not as one grudgingly given. Remember this: Whoever sows sparingly will also reap sparingly, and whoever sows generously will also reap generously. Each man should give what he has decided in his heart to give, not reluctantly or under compulsion, for God loves a cheerful giver. And God is able to make all grace abound to you, so that in all things at all times, having all that you need, you will abound in every good work." (2 Corinthians 9:5–8)

• Give generously and openhandedly toward the needy.

"Give generously to [the needy] and do so without a grudging heart; then because of this the LORD your God will bless you in all your work and in everything you put your hand to. There will always be poor people in the land. Therefore I command you to be openhanded toward your brothers and toward the poor and needy in your land." (Deuteronomy 15:10–11)

• Give secretly.

"So when you give to the needy, do not announce it with trumpets, as the hypocrites do in the synagogues and on the streets, to be honored by men. I tell you the truth, they have received their reward in full. But when you give to the needy, do not let your left hand know what your right hand is doing, so that your giving may be in secret. Then your Father, who sees what is done in secret, will reward you." (Matthew 6:2–4)

• Give humbly.

"To some who were confident of their own righteousness and looked down on everybody else, Jesus told this parable: 'Two men went up to the temple to pray, one a Pharisee and the other a tax collector. The Pharisee stood up and prayed about himself: "God, I thank you that I am not like other men—robbers, evildoers, adulterers—or even like this tax collector. I fast twice a week and give a tenth of all I get."

But the tax collector stood at a distance. He would not even look up to heaven, but beat his breast and said, "God, have mercy on me, a sinner." I tell you that this man, rather than the other, went home justified before God. For everyone who exalts himself will be humbled, and he who humbles himself will be exalted.'" (Luke 18:9–14)

• Give back to God what is rightfully His.

"So the spies questioned him: 'Teacher, we know that you speak and teach what is right, and that you do not show partiality but teach the way of God in accordance with the truth. Is it right for us to pay taxes to Caesar or not?'

"He saw through their duplicity and said to them, 'Show me a denarius. Whose portrait and inscription are on it?'

"'Caesar's,' they replied.

"He said to them, 'Then give to Caesar what is Caesar's, and to God what is God's.' (Luke 20:21–25)

• Give sacrificially.

"Jesus sat down opposite the place where the offerings were put and watched the crowd putting their money into the temple treasury. Many rich people threw in large amounts. But a poor widow came and put in two very small copper coins, worth only a fraction of a penny.

"Calling his disciples to him, Jesus said, 'I tell you the truth, this poor widow has put more into the treasury than all the others. They all gave out of their wealth; but she, out of her poverty, put in everything—all she had to live on.'" (Mark 12:41–44)

Prayer for Today

God, thank You for making all grace abound to my children. Thank You for providing everything they need to abound in every good work. Thank You that You provide everything possible for my children to give to others. I pray that You will enlarge their hearts to be generous on every occasion and that their generosity will result in others' thanksgiving to You. Amen.

Based on 2 Corinthians 9:8–11

Reflections

1. What obstacles do your children face with being generous?
2. How can you help your children understand the effect their gifts could have for good?
3. Other than money, what else could your children be generous with?
4. Think about a time you gave generously. How did God use your gift for good?

"And now, brothers, we want you to know about the grace that God has given the Macedonian churches. Out of the most severe trial, their overflowing joy and their extreme poverty welled up in rich generosity. For I testify that they gave as much as they were able, and even beyond their ability. Entirely on their own, they urgently pleaded with us for the privilege of sharing in this service to the saints. And they did not do as we expected, but they gave themselves first to the Lord and then to us in keeping with God's will."

—2 Corinthians 8:1–5

23

GRAVEN IMAGES

"Before him all the nations are as nothing; they are regarded by him as worthless and less than nothing. To whom, then, will you compare God? What image will you compare him to?"
—ISAIAH 40:17–18

When I was on the staff of a college ministry many years ago, we took a spring break mission trip to Los Angeles. Part of that trip included a day-long tour of the city's multicultural and religious diversity. At one of our stops, we visited a Hare Krishna temple. As we stepped off our buses, several devotees greeted us and offered us food. I declined their offer. Yet once in the temple, I noticed that my shoe was untied and knelt to tie it.

After we left, I searched my heart to determine if I had just bowed my knee to an idol. How could I have allowed such a thing? For some time, I was troubled by the thought that I had in some way inadvertently worshiped an idol.

Yet God, in His goodness, helped me understand that this was an innocent act—not an act of worship. In the same way, the things that capture our children's attention—and perhaps too much of our attention—can become idols when several characteristics are present.

Perhaps we as parents need to curb our kids' involvement in certain things, but to remain true to the Word of God, we need to be careful that we are not calling something an idol if it isn't.

Ezekiel 14:2–3a stumped me for a while as I studied "idols" in the Bible. It says, "Then the word of the LORD came to me: 'Son of man, these men have set up idols in their hearts and put wicked stumbling blocks before their faces.'"

I wondered what God meant by saying someone "put wicked stumbling blocks before [his face]." My family and I discussed all the things that could be "wicked stumbling blocks," such as sports, video games, entertainment, even hobbies. Of course, I thought about all the worthless stuff on television these days, and I wondered if that's one thing God is talking about. Do we need to get rid of our TV? Maybe. Do we need to limit our exposure to television? Definitely! But not for reasons of idolatry, in my opinion. And I'll tell you why—because TV passed the test for us.

What—if anything—can you think of that may have become an idol in your child's life? Think of that thing as you take the following test to see if it too can pass the test. If you or one of your family members answers yes to any question, it should raise concerns to pray over and discuss.

Idolatry Quiz

"Put to death, therefore, whatever belongs to your earthly nature: sexual immorality, impurity, lust, evil desires and greed, which is idolatry. Because of these, the wrath of God is coming." (Colossians 3:5–6)

• Is the potential idol a form of sexual immorality, impurity, or lust?

• Is it a form of evil desire or greed?

"Then the word of the LORD came to me: 'Son of man, these men have set up idols in their hearts and put wicked stumbling blocks before their faces. Should I let them inquire of me at all? Therefore speak to them and tell them, "This is what the Sovereign LORD says: When any Israelite sets up idols in his heart and puts a wicked stumbling block before his face and then goes to a prophet, I the LORD will answer him myself in keeping with his great idolatry. I will do this to recapture the hearts of the people of Israel, who have all deserted me for their idols."'" (Ezekiel 14:2–5)

• Is the thing in question an obstacle to your child's worship of God?

• Does it separate your child from God?

"For since the creation of the world God's invisible qualities—his eternal power and divine nature—have been clearly seen, being understood from what has been made, so that men are without excuse. For although they knew God, they neither glorified him as God nor gave thanks to him, but their thinking became futile and their foolish hearts were darkened. Although they claimed to be wise, they became fools and exchanged the glory of the immortal God for images made to look like mortal man and birds and animals and reptiles.

"Therefore God gave them over in the sinful desires of their hearts to sexual impurity for the degrading of their bodies with one another. They exchanged the truth of God for a lie, and worshiped and served created things rather than the Creator—who is forever praised. Amen." (Romans 1:20–25)

• Does it keep your child from honoring, glorifying, or magnifying God?

- Does it stand in the way of your child's gratitude toward God?
- Does involvement in this activity or with this thing cause your child to reject the truth and instead believe a lie?
- Does your child worship, venerate, or adore this activity or thing?
- Is this the most important thing in your child's life?

"Be careful not to forget the covenant of the LORD your God that he made with you; do not make for yourselves an idol in the form of anything the LORD your God has forbidden. For the LORD your God is a consuming fire, a jealous God." (Deuteronomy 4:23–24)

- Has this activity or thing caused your child to forget his or her covenant with God?
- Is this something that God has forbidden?

"They exchanged their Glory for an image of a bull, which eats grass. They forgot the God who saved them, who had done great things in Egypt, miracles in the land of Ham and awesome deeds by the Red Sea. . . . They yoked themselves to the Baal of Peor and ate sacrifices offered to lifeless gods. . . . They worshiped their idols, which became a snare to them. They sacrificed their sons and their daughters to demons. They shed innocent blood, the blood of their sons and daughters, whom they sacrificed to the idols of Canaan, and the land was desecrated by their blood. They defiled themselves by what they did; by their deeds they prostituted themselves. . . . He handed them over to the nations, and their foes ruled over them." (Psalm 106:20–22, 28, 36–39, 41)

- Does this activity or thing make your child forget God?
- Does your child seem to be yoked, in bondage to, or unduly connected to this activity or thing?

• Has this activity or thing become a snare to your child, and does it seem to have power over your child?

• Does involvement in this activity or thing seem to cause your child to make irrational or even ungodly decisions for the sake of it?

"Of what value is an idol, since a man has carved it? Or an image that teaches lies? For he who makes it trusts in his own creation; he makes idols that cannot speak. Woe to him who says to wood, 'Come to life!' Or to lifeless stone, 'Wake up!' Can it give guidance? It is covered with gold and silver; there is no breath in it." (Habakkuk 2:18–19)

• Does your child seem to seek guidance from this activity or thing?

If you answered "yes" to any of the above questions, discuss your concerns with your spouse. Pray about limiting your child's involvement with the thing in question. Remember that the overarching filter is that your child has begun to worship the thing in question. Read the quiz Scriptures with your child and have your child take this quiz. Ask God to give you guidance as you try to discern how to best help your child.

Prayer for Today

God, apart from You, my children have no good thing. I pray that You would put it in their hearts every day to want to bring honor to You. Help them see and understand that Yours is the only kingdom worth living for. Amen.

Based on Ezra 7:27

Reflections

1. Has God ever dealt with you regarding something that had become an idol in your life? If so, explain.
2. Did this quiz clarify any of your questions regarding idolatry?

Why or why not?

3. Why do you think God is jealous of false gods?

Family Exercise

Try this exercise for anything your family identifies as a potential idol for them. Declare a weeklong fast from that thing. Discuss any signs of "withdrawal" and any bonds that may be broken during that week.

"Be careful, or you will be enticed to turn away and worship other gods and bow down to them. Then the LORD's anger will burn against you, and he will shut the heavens so that it will not rain and the ground will yield no produce, and you will soon perish from the good land the LORD is giving you."

—*Deuteronomy 11:16–17*

24

CHOOSE LIFE

"When Moses finished reciting all these words to all Israel, he said to them, 'Take to heart all the words I have solemnly declared to you this day, so that you may command your children to obey carefully all the words of this law. They are not just idle words for you—they are your life. By them you will live long in the land you are crossing the Jordan to possess.'"
—DEUTERONOMY 32:45–47

One day in the car, Abby asked if she could get her tongue pierced when she's older. Abby was six, so at that point in our lives, thank God, this was her curiosity talking, rather than her will.

"I don't know," I began, and I saw Mike tighten his grip on the steering wheel. He gave me that "just say no!" look in the rearview mirror. That would be too easy! And besides, it wouldn't help our children think biblically if we simply delivered a mandate. I flashed one of those "just trust me" smiles right back at him from the middle seat of our Suburban.

"Let's think about what God's Word says about piercing our bodies," I said and then fumbled around in my mental Scripture archives and couldn't think of anything right off. Mike didn't offer any words of truth either.

"Well," I continued, "let's take a look at Philippians 4:8 and evaluate body-piercing with that Scripture."

Our kids (eleven, six, and four) were all ears!

"'Whatever is pure . . .' is it pure? Well, that's what we're not sure of," I mused and caught another of Mike's looks.

"'Whatever is lovely . . .' is it lovely?" I asked. "Hmmm, I'm not sure."

"OK, what about 'whatever is of good report'? Do you think people who have pierced tongues have a good reputation?"

"No!" my kids piped in. Mike's knuckles relaxed.

"They may be great people, but you're right. Others may not think they have a good reputation at first. So I'd say that God isn't really for body piercing," I summed up our impromptu Bible study.

I leaned back, proud of the fact that we'd captured a moment to help our children evaluate tongue-piercing with the Word of God. Mike and I gave each other that self-satisfied "aren't we good parents?" look that Abby immediately shattered.

"Well," she said, "when I move away from home, I can do whatever I want."

"Yes, you can," I shot back and then desperately pleaded, "but I hope you'll do what's pleasing to God!"

It's true. She can do whatever she wants—and I'm convinced that she *will* do whatever *she* wants—if her heart is not wholly devoted to God. This incident made Mike and me think hard about this question: How can we effectively train and nurture our children to love God with all their heart when they hold in their hearts the ability to reject all that we teach them, pray for them, and strive to pass on to them?

Their free will—their ability to choose—is a primary key for our children to love God with all their heart. It's even more important than what we do!

Yes, we need to train our children to love God. We need to be faithful to obey the things that God has revealed to us in training our children. And yet, even after we've done everything we can do, they may choose not to follow God or to love Him. We have to understand that we have a role, God's work in our children's hearts has a role, and ultimately their response has a role. We cannot control our children's response to God. We can only control our faithfulness to do what God has told us to do in guiding their hearts.

Then what *can* we do to make the choice of following God and loving Him with all their heart so appealing to our children? Scripture reveals several secrets to do just that.

Deuteronomy 30:19–20 says,

> This day I call heaven and earth as witnesses against you that I have set before you life and death, blessings and curses. Now choose life, so that you and your children may live and that you may love the LORD your God, listen to his voice, and hold fast to him. For the LORD is your life, and he will give you many years in the land he swore to give to your fathers, Abraham, Isaac and Jacob.

These verses set out clearly that God has extended a choice—life or death, blessings or curses. We can explain to our children that if they choose God, they choose life.

From Deuteronomy 30:19–20, we need to guide our children in three areas: to love the Lord, listen to His voice, and hold fast to Him.

• **Love the Lord.** John 14:21 says, "Whoever has my commands and obeys them, he is the one who loves me. He who loves me will be loved by my Father, and I too will love him and show myself to him." That's an incredible promise for our children—that Christ will love them and show Himself to them! But the prerequisite for Christ showing Himself—other than a personal relationship with Him—is that they must demonstrate their love for Christ by obeying Him. If you love Me, you will obey Me, Jesus says.

• **Listen to His voice.** To be a friend of Jesus is a worthy goal for every person, but especially for our children. How is that possible? Jesus says in John 15:14–15, "You are my friends *if you do what I command.* I no longer call you servants, because a servant does not know his master's business. Instead, I have called you friends, for everything that I learned from my Father I have made known to you" (italics added). God has been faithful to reveal to our children what He requires of them. Their responsibility is to be faithful to obey what He has spoken to them.

• **Hold fast to Him.** In Deuteronomy 11:26–28, God says, "See, I am setting before you today a blessing and a curse—the blessing if you obey the commands of the LORD your God that I am giving you today; the curse if you disobey the commands of the LORD your God and turn from the way that I command you today by following other gods, which you have not known." God calls our children to forsake all other gods or substitutions for Him. They need to understand that they have no life apart from the life that is in Him alone. We need to encourage our children to hold fast to God by obeying Him.

Ultimately in all three of these areas, the central theme is obedience. But what is the proper motivation for this obedience? We can demand obedience from our children by laying down God's laws and holding them to those laws. Yet without a full understanding of *why* they should obey, our children will strive to break out of this legalistic box as soon as they are old enough to do so. Or they will attempt to obey the laws and wrongly think that by doing so they will earn favor with God—again, knowing the reason for the Law is crucial. And the biblical *reason* is to show us God's holiness and let us see that we cannot keep God's law without God's aid. Thus, we need Christ, and only His Holy Spirit can give us the ability to obey God's law.

We need to introduce our children to a loving God who longs to give them a full and abundant life. And day by day, as a family, we need to walk in the grace that His love brings to us. Second Corinthians 7:1 admonishes us that "since we have these promises, dear friends, let us purify ourselves from everything that contaminates body and spirit, perfecting holiness out of reverence for God." If we get stuck on the response part of this verse—purifying ourselves and perfecting holiness—we may alienate our children by pounding them with the Law rather than extending to them a loving relationship to elicit their obedience.

What are the promises 2 Corinthians 7:1 refers to? Those are listed in the previous verses in 2 Corinthians 6:16–18:

> What agreement is there between the temple of God and idols? For we are the temple of the living God. As God has said: "I will live with them and walk among them, and I will be their God, and they will be my people. Therefore come out from them and be separate, says the Lord. Touch no unclean thing, and I will receive you. I will be a Father to you, and you will be my sons and daughters, says the Lord Almighty."

The promises are about a wonderful loving relationship with our Creator. God promises to

- live with us and walk among us,
- be our God and for us to be His people,
- receive us, and
- be a Father to us.

The promises are about relationship!

So, back to my tongue-piercing-question ordeal with Abby. We need to explain our stance on issues and what we perceive to be God's revealed truth. Yet more than anything else, we need to continue to introduce our children to a loving Savior and God who alone can develop in them an intimate love relationship that will result in ongoing obedience.

Prayer for Today

God, I pray that my children will obey Your commands, decrees, and laws. I pray that as long as my children live they will demonstrate their reverence for You by obeying You. Thank You for the promise of long life—everlasting life—that You give us. Amen.

Based on Deuteronomy 6:2

Reflections

1. How does it make you feel to know that you can't control your child's response to God? Explain.
2. How will this understanding affect your prayers for your children?
3. List the most appealing things about your relationship with God that you could share with your children.
4. Give yourself a score from 1 to 10 (1= not at all; 10= wholeheartedly) in these three areas: loving God, listening to God, and holding fast to God. What—if anything—do you need to do differently in any of these three areas?

"Teach me, O LORD, to follow your decrees; then I will keep them to the end. Give me understanding, and I will keep your law and obey it with all my heart. Direct me in the path of your commands, for there I find delight."

—Psalm 119:33–35

25

STAND FIRM

"Be on your guard; stand firm in the faith;
be men of courage; be strong."
—I CORINTHIANS 16:13

If anyone knows what it is to be fearful, it's parents today. We have a culture of extreme fearfulness. I am not sure why we are a fearful lot of parents, but I have my theories. Perhaps we are more fearful than our parents were because we live in an information age where we know more about all the things that could go wrong and harm our children. Or perhaps, thanks to the Columbine-like incidents, acts of terrorism, and the accounts of child abductions, we fear a world that seems to be spinning out of control with evil.

It's difficult to be parents who can swallow our fears and encourage our children to do the courageous thing when we want desperately to protect them. I remember seeing a cartoon once about overprotective parents. Inside a van was an alarm that would go off if the child wasn't safely buckled in. The child wore a bike helmet and pads to protect him from injury. The van was fitted with a Breathalyzer to test against drug and alcohol use. And the walls were padded.

The point, well taken, is that parents today tend to buy every gadget to protect their children. Neil Howe and William Strauss, authors of *The Fourth Turning,* say that this millennial generation (children born from 1980 on) is a protected generation.

What is the result of such protection? The first result is a positive one. This generation of children sees itself as valued and protected, and that results in a positive idealism. They figure they must be worth a lot for there to be so much fuss about keeping them safe.

The second result is not so positive. As parents model fearfulness toward a hostile environment that may harm or even kill these precious children, children also learn to be fearful.

I admit that I am one of the protective parents who has difficulty saying, "Go ahead and do it! Trust God!" Yet I know that I need to grow in this area. If I continue to model fearfulness for my children, I will infect them with a paralysis of action and faith that results from fear.

God calls our children to be courageous rather than fearful. The Bible talks a great deal about trusting in God rather than fearing man. So often, we allow our fear of what people can do to our children to keep us from seeing God do wonders on their behalf.

The fear of people is more than just fearing the harm they can do to our children. Its more insidious manifestation is in an exaggerated concern over what people will think of our children.

I grew up in an age when "what will people think?" was foremost on our parents' minds. The tragic result is that insecurity and people-pleasing tendencies have dogged me since childhood. If we as parents don't understand what our fear of people can do to our children, they also will face challenges in getting their eyes off themselves and onto loving God with all their heart.

Proverbs 29:25 says that the "fear of man will prove to be a snare, but whoever trusts in the LORD is kept safe." If our children are taught to fear others, their fear will make it difficult for them to speak out boldly for God. Their fear will also make it difficult for them to obey God with all their heart when He asks them to take a risk and do a scary thing.

The other day in the car, we were at a Sonic Drive-In. I was in the front seat, concentrating on writing this book. I noticed a man with a grocery cart full of items sitting at a table in front of our car, but I kept working. Grant, however, did not merely notice the man, but watched him intently.

"I want to give that homeless man some money," Grant said. At first, I wasn't listening to him. But after he said something to that effect a couple more times, I listened.

"Mom, would it be OK if I bought that man's dinner?" he asked.

Normally, my "what would people think?" and "he might reject you and hurt you" filters would have kicked in. But I'm learning from the Bible study I'm doing for this book, so I responded differently.

"It's your choice, Grant. What do you want to do?" I asked.

Grant watched the man a little longer. He decided that the man wasn't homeless, just a little scruffy. Grant didn't want to embarrass the man, so he chose to stay in the car.

That was a victory for me! I moved beyond my fear of people and released my son to listen to and obey God. That's an important lesson for me, because every time we see someone in need, Grant wants to help. One time he tried to give away his baseball cap to a homeless man sleeping on a steam grate in Washington, D.C. If I give in to my fears at those times, I run the risk of squelching the incredible work that God is doing in my son to give him a sensitive, caring heart that results in action.

Each time we as parents are able to release our children, we allow God to build a record of success with them. God is actively working in His children's lives to teach them to trust Him. Each time our children trust God and see Him work, they can remember later what God has done and trust Him again.

When God led the Israelites out of Egypt, He performed miraculous wonders in protecting them. Yet after God performed those wonders, the Israelites' fears often kept them from trusting God. Over and over, God reminded them of what He had done so they would trust Him, such as in Deuteronomy 1:29–33:

> Then I said to you, "Do not be terrified; do not be afraid of them. The LORD your God, who is going before you, will fight for you, as he did for you in Egypt, before your very eyes, and in the desert. There you saw how the LORD your God carried you, as a father carries his son, all the way you went until you reached this place. In spite of this, you did not trust in the LORD your God, who went ahead of you on your journey, in fire by night and in a cloud by day, to search out places for you to camp and to show you the way you should go."

God longs to build a track record of His amazing power with our children, so their faith in Him will grow exponentially! We must not stand in the way of that because of our fears. Our children need to be encouraged to trust God. Psalm 20:7–8 says, "Some trust in chariots and some in horses, but we trust in the name of the LORD our God. They are brought to their knees and fall, but we rise up and stand firm."

Our children need to obey God rather than worrying about what people think. After Peter and the apostles were delivered from jail in Acts 5, they were brought before the Sanhedrin. The leaders in Acts 5:28 said, "We gave you strict orders not to teach in this name. . . . Yet you have filled Jerusalem with your teaching and are determined to make us guilty of this man's blood."

What did Peter and the other apostles reply? "We must obey God rather than men!"

Second Corinthians 1:21–22 says, "Now it is God who makes both us and you stand firm in Christ. He anointed us, set his seal of ownership on us, and put his Spirit in our hearts as a deposit, guaranteeing what is to come." Verse 24 says that "it is by faith you stand firm"!

God is calling our children as He is calling all children and adults who are His to stand firm for Him. We need to understand that it is God alone who can make us and our children stand firm. It is not a work of the flesh that we just hang tough and do this. Our role in this is by faith to choose to stand firm and allow God to help us do so.

Prayer for Today

God, I pray for my children that they will stand firm and hold to Your teachings. I pray that the Lord Jesus Christ Himself and God our Father, who loved us and by His grace gave us eternal encouragement and good hope, would encourage my children's hearts and strengthen them in every good deed and word. Amen.

Based on 2 Thessalonians 2:15–17

Reflections

1. What are you afraid of for your children? How do you deal with that fear?
2. In what ways might your fears be negatively affecting your children's faith in God?
3. Think of each of your children. What is it that each child fears most? Which of the fears could stand in the way of that child trusting God with all his or her heart?
4. With your family, create a list of all the ways God has protected your family. Celebrate God's track record of faithfulness for your family.

Family Exercise

Play this game with your family to help them understand "standing firm." Place a sheet of paper on the floor for each person in your family. Have each family member stand on a sheet of paper. Adjust the placement of the papers so each person is a couple inches less than arm's length from one another.

Tell everyone that the goal of the game is to stand firm on the paper. On "go," have family members do everything they can to knock each other off the paper, while staying on their own paper.

After a couple minutes or when everyone is knocked off, talk about the things they're afraid of that can keep them from standing firm. For each fear, brainstorm ways that each person can trust God. Have each family member write those things on his or her sheet of paper (or a clean one) as a reminder to trust God. Each person can hang this paper in his or her room.

"God is our refuge and strength, an ever-present help in trouble. Therefore we will not fear, though the earth give way and the mountains fall into the heart of the sea, though its waters roar and foam and the mountains quake with their surging. . . . 'Be still, and know that I am God; I will be exalted among the nations, I will be exalted in the earth.' The LORD Almighty is with us; the God of Jacob is our fortress."

—Psalm 46:1–3, 10–11

26

TALK TO ME

"Ask and it will be given to you; seek and you will find; knock and the door will be opened to you. For everyone who asks receives; he who seeks finds; and to him who knocks, the door will be opened."
—MATTHEW 7:7–8

When my husband, Mike, was eight years old, there was nothing he wanted more than a new bicycle. He had even picked out the very bike he wanted at the store, and it cost $125; Mike, however, had no money.

One evening in the wintertime, he lay on his bed and prayed, "God, I'll do anything. I just want a bike. I want a bike."

As Mike prayed, he felt as though the Spirit of God came over him, and his prayer changed from a selfish prayer to a submissive prayer. He prayed, "God, show me *how* to get a bike."

To this day, Mike remembers God impressing him with this thought: *I will help you get a bike.* Mike was filled with a sense of peace that God had answered his prayer. He was also awestruck because this was the first time anything like this had ever happened to him.

Mike feels that God gave him the strength and the discipline to save his allowance. Mike did odd jobs around the house to make extra money. He also worked at his family's store to make extra money. Although Mike watched his sisters spend their money on candy, he was able to hold on to the money God had enabled him to earn. He saved more than one hundred dollars.

Mike's father was so proud of him that he paid the last twenty-five dollars, enabling Mike to buy his dream bike that summer. Now Mike tells that story often to our children as an encouragement to trust God to hear and answer their prayers.

The practice of prayer is one of the easiest things for us parents to teach our children. It seems that from birth, children are able to trust in a God that they cannot see. They watch as we model bowing our heads and saying grace before meals. They pray with us at bedtime. They seem to know innately that God is listening.

Children who regularly see their parents cry out to God for their needs and pray to God for those they love are children who often pray as well. One of the practices our family has is praying when we hear a siren. We pray for safety for the people who are going to help someone who is hurting. We pray for the person who is needing care, that God will sustain the person's life and bring healing. We pray for everyone involved that God will pour out His grace and that somehow God will be glorified. Now whenever we hear a siren, it's our children who think to pray and who often lead us in prayer.

First Thessalonians 5:17 admonishes us to "pray continually." Praying continually has the sense of an incessant cough—the kind of cough that just won't seem to go away. This Scripture isn't saying that we need to pray every second and never take a break. Rather, it's saying that the prayer lines need to be open all day long as we pray regularly. So, throughout the day, we are to pray about everything as we are in constant communion with God.

I asked my children one day in the car when they pray. My oldest child's answer alarmed me. "When I'm afraid and before meals," Grant said.

"Is that the only time you pray, Grant?" I asked.

"Pretty much."

"You don't pray at school or when you have a test or anything?" I asked.

"Nope."

That was a wake-up call for me to be more intentional in helping my children understand that prayer is their open invitation to talk to the living God. But why is prayer such a vital ingredient for children to learn to love God with all their heart?

For one thing, when we pray for something, we give our heart to the cause. Second Corinthians 9:14 says, "And in their prayers for you *their hearts will go out to you,* because of the surpassing grace God has given you" (italics added).

Some people say that prayer changes the pray-er more than it changes God. There's a bit of truth in that statement. Prayer does change our hearts as our hearts go out to the ones we're praying for, but if the only thing prayer is for is to change us, what's the point?

Scripture is full of assurances of answered prayer if we only pray. If prayer does nothing to change the course of things, then we shouldn't waste our time or our children's time on its futility.

Prayer is not futile. Take a look at these promises for answered prayer.

• "Jesus replied, 'I tell you the truth, if you have faith and do not doubt, not only can you do what was done to the fig tree, but also you can say to this mountain, "Go, throw yourself into the sea," and it will be done. If you believe, you will receive whatever you ask for in prayer.'" (Matthew 21:21–22)

• "I tell you the truth, whatever you bind on earth will be bound in heaven, and whatever you loose on earth will be loosed in heaven. Again, I tell you that if two of you on earth agree about anything you ask for, it will be done for you by my Father in heaven." (Matthew 18:18–19)

God answers prayer, but He answers prayer in three ways: yes, no, and wait. When God answers yes, it boosts our faith and may tempt us to think that we have a blank check for God to sign for anything we want. That happened to our son Reed several summers ago.

We were making our annual trek to Oklahoma to visit my parents and extended family. We knew that our Plymouth Voyager van was not in the best condition, but we figured it would at least get us to Oklahoma and back to Colorado one more time.

Halfway across Kansas, though, we discovered we were wrong. First of all, the speedometer broke so we couldn't tell how fast we were going. That wasn't too big an issue, however, because whenever we got to what seemed to be around 40 mph, the entire vehicle shook as though it were going to fall apart. A sixteen-hour trip was beginning to look like a twenty-four-hour trip because of how slow we needed to go. Cars zoomed past us as we crept along.

Finally, we pulled off the highway to get some mechanical help in town. We found a dealer but discovered that it would be hours before the mechanics could even look at our car—and then there was no guarantee they could help us. We piled back in the car and shimmied back onto the highway.

"We need to pray," I said. And we did.

I don't even remember what we prayed exactly, but miraculously the car stopped shaking as we approached higher speeds. God fixed our car! And it did not shake the rest of the trip!

When we were convinced that the car was fixed, we thanked God for His faithfulness to us. Each of us prayed and celebrated what a great God we have.

At the end of the prayer, Reed, who was three at the time, piped in, "And, God, I want a four-wheeler and a new bike. . . ."

Whoa there, fella!

Even with all the promises for answered prayer in Scripture, there are requirements also, such as being persistent in prayer (Luke 11:5–10), forgiving others before we pray (Matthew 5:23–24), and believing when we pray (Matthew 21:22).

We need to be careful that we don't communicate to our children that God is some kind of big Santa Claus in the sky who will give us anything and everything we ask for. Even as they ask us for things, as parents we have the big picture and we understand that some things they ask for may not be to their benefit. Their loving heavenly Father also knows what is best for them, and the answer may need to be no.

After the issue of answered and unanswered prayer, there are three key principles related to prayer and our hearts that we need to teach our children.

1. Prayer helps us get real before God. Our children need to understand that it's impossible to fake it when they talk to God. God already knows their hearts. Because of that, our children can talk to God without "high and mighty" church language. They can simply be real before God and talk to Him with respect, but as though they are talking to a friend.

2. Sin hinders our prayers. To piggyback on the first point, we cannot pretend that we have no sin in our lives when we really do. Unconfessed sin is like a bad telephone connection that fills our prayers with static. Lamentations 3:40–44 illustrates this by saying,

Let us examine our ways and test them, and let us return to the LORD. Let us lift up our hearts and our hands to God in heaven, and say: "We have sinned and rebelled and you have not forgiven. You have covered yourself with anger and pursued us; you have slain without pity. You have covered yourself with a cloud so that no prayer can get through."

3. We should pour out our hearts to God. How can we teach our children this? There is nothing more powerful than modeling. I love to hear children of praying parents pray. You can hear the intonations their parents use and even the same phrases. We need to pray with our children in genuine ways. When we pray as a family, our children learn more than they will ever learn about prayer by doing a Bible study on prayer, memorizing verses about prayer, or reading a book about prayer.

Having gotten more intentional about praying with our children, we were very pleased the other day. A woman in our church had just been sentenced to prison. We were having lunch when I said that we needed to be praying for her. Grant said, "I prayed for her this morning." And Abby said, "I prayed while you were talking." Praise God!

Prayer changes the world, and it also changes our children's hearts. We have a tremendous opportunity to model for our children a vibrant prayer life. As they too develop a vibrant prayer life, God will capture their hearts.

Prayer for Today

God, I pray that You would direct my children's hearts into Your love and Christ's perseverance as they learn to pray continually to You. Amen.

Based on 2 Thessalonians 3:5

Reflections

1. How would you rate your personal prayer life on the scale below?

1	2	3	4	5
Anemic				Robust
(needs a dose of power)			(thriving and powerful)	

2. For each of your children, rate his or her prayer life according to the scale above. What insight does this give you about your children?
3. List answers to prayer that you've seen in the last month. What does this list reflect about your prayer life? What, if any, changes do you need to make to what you're modeling for your children in prayer?
4. What is your greatest motivation to pray?
5. Discuss with your family things in your life—such as the sound of sirens—that can prompt your family to pray for others.

Family Exercise

Use this object lesson to help your children learn about pouring out their hearts to God.

Have your children pour out the water in a pitcher until it's empty. Then discuss with them what happened to the water and what's left in the pitcher.

Read aloud Lamentations 2:19: "Arise, cry out in the night, as the watches of the night begin; pour out your heart like water in the presence of the Lord. Lift up your hands to him for the lives of your children, who faint from hunger at the head of every street."

Help your children make connections with these questions: "What happened to the water? What does God mean when He says in the Bible to pour out our hearts to Him? After we've poured out our hearts to God, what will our hearts be like?"

"I call on you, O God, for you will answer me; give ear to me and hear my prayer. Show the wonder of your great love, you who save by your right hand those who take refuge in you from their foes. Keep me as the apple of your eye; hide me in the shadow of your wings."

—*Psalm 17:6–8*

27
CRYSTAL CLEAR

"He who loves a pure heart and whose speech is gracious will have the king for his friend."
—PROVERBS 22:11

Our son Grant has one of the purest hearts of any child I know. While we were staying at my husband's aunt's house over Labor Day weekend last year, I saw this more clearly than ever.

Grant, eleven, was assigned to sleep on the couch in the living room. He had turned on the television and was channel surfing before he went to sleep. The TV was complete with cable and no child-screens, which we weren't aware of yet.

Mike and I were already asleep when Grant came into our room. "Mom, wake up." He was crying and shaken.

"Mom, I was watching TV and a naked person was on it. I didn't mean to," he sobbed.

I held him and comforted him. I assured him that this wasn't his fault and he had done the right thing to turn it off immediately. When he had calmed down and gone back to bed (without

TV), I marveled at his pure heart.

Psalm 73:1 says, "Surely God is good to Israel, to those who are *pure* in heart" (italics added). This verse emphasizes the benefit of loving God with all our heart. So what does it mean to be pure in heart?

I remember a sermon our youth pastor gave about being pure in heart. He listed the bare minimum requirements for the purity of the food we eat. Did you know that according to the Food and Drug Administration it's OK for a certain number of rat hairs to be present in our food? The same is true with a maximum of finger-nail or insect pieces in foods that are allowable to pass inspection.

Of course, these are maximums. It wouldn't be permissible for a food to be filled with rat hair, but one or two hairs will pass inspection.

How does that make you feel? Makes you want to gag, huh?

With God, there are no maximums or minimums when it comes to purity of heart. God wants ours and our children's hearts to be clean, clear, and pure. The standard is high, yet the reward is even higher—God's goodness, blessing, and favor on our children.

Let me stop here to talk about the difference between works and grace. Absolutely, without a shadow of a doubt, salvation is a gift from God. It is unmerited favor bestowed on us by a gracious and loving God through the death and resurrection of His Son. And, when we are in Christ, there is a positional purity that is given to all believers. Romans 8:1 says, "Therefore, there is now no condemnation for those who are in Christ Jesus." When God looks at us as believers, we are clothed in the purity of Christ.

And yet, we are called to grow in that righteousness on a prac-tical day-to-day basis. Romans 8:4 says that the righteous require-ments of the Law are to be fully met in us by Christ's sacrifice and our walking according to the Spirit instead of our natural self.

Romans 8:7 says that "the sinful mind is hostile to God. It does not submit to God's law, nor can it do so." Romans 8:13 challenges us that "if you live according to the sinful nature, you will die; but if by the Spirit you put to death the misdeeds of the body, you will live."

When our children believe in Jesus Christ as their Savior, they are fully justified before God. Just like us, though, they need to appropriate all that they've received from Christ by living lives that honor Him—by loving Him with pure hearts.

What does it mean to have a pure heart? Let's take a look at Psalm 101:2–8:

> I will be careful to lead a blameless life—when will you come to me? I will walk in my house with blameless heart. I will set before my eyes no vile thing. The deeds of faithless men I hate; they will not cling to me. Men of perverse heart shall be far from me; I will have nothing to do with evil. Whoever slanders his neighbor in secret, him will I put to silence; whoever has haughty eyes and a proud heart, him will I not endure. My eyes will be on the faithful in the land, that they may dwell with me; he whose walk is blameless will minister to me. No one who practices deceit will dwell in my house; no one who speaks falsely will stand in my presence. Every morning I will put to silence all the wicked in the land; I will cut off every evildoer from the city of the LORD.

In this passage, the psalmist illumines two key influences on a pure heart. The first is the area of input, and the second is the area of associations. In the area of input, the psalmist writes

- I will set before my eyes no vile thing.
- My eyes will be on the faithful in the land, that they may dwell with me.

Are there any things in your children's lives that would qual-

169

ify as a "vile thing"? For us, television is filled with vile things. Yes, we have a television, but we limit what the children see, and we monitor what they watch. We tried cable TV for a month and got more exposure to vile things than we ever dreamed of. Are television shows, movies, books, magazines, video games, or music serving as vile things in your children's lives?

What involvement do your children have with other Christians? Are you intentional about plugging them into worship, Sunday school, youth groups, mission trips, and more at your church? These are great ways to expose your children to others who love God.

In the area of associations, the psalmist writes

• Men of perverse heart shall be far from me; I will have nothing to do with evil.
• Whoever slanders his neighbor in secret, him will I not put to silence.
• He whose walk is blameless will minister to me.
• No one who practices deceit will dwell in my house; no one who speaks falsely will stand in my presence.
• I will cut off every evildoer from the city of the Lord.

What is your children's attitude toward those who do evil? You can tell by what burdens or troubles them when they're around people who don't love God. Grant went to middle school this year—his first year. And it hasn't been a pleasant experience for him. Kids who curse and make nasty gestures drive him crazy. This toxic environment has served to pull his morale down as he has to fight the bad associations' influence day in and day out. Mike and I are considering ways we can lessen his time at school and thus his exposure to ungodliness.

The amazing promise for children who monitor the input and associations they have is found in this passage:

Come and listen, all you who fear God; let me tell you what he has done for me. I cried out to him with my mouth; his praise was on my tongue. If I had cherished sin in my heart, the Lord would not have listened; but God has surely listened and heard my voice in prayer. Praise be to God, who has not rejected my prayer or withheld his love from me! (Psalm 66:16–20)

When our children pursue having pure hearts before God, the God of the universe will make His ear attentive to them.

Prayer for Today

God, I pray that You would help my children flee the evil desires of youth. Instead, I pray that You would give them a heart to pursue righteousness, faith, love, and peace, along with those who call on You out of a pure heart. Amen.

Based on 2 Timothy 2:22

Reflections

1. What is the difference between our positional purity before God and our daily pursuit of a pure heart?
2. What is the difference between works and grace?
3. Why do you think input and associations can defile our children's hearts?

Family Exercise

To help your children understand the concept of a pure heart, use this object lesson. You'll need a glass of water, food coloring, and a cup of bleach.

As you name things that can defile our hearts, drop food coloring into the water so it will be murky. Then tell children that God can forgive us of our impurities and allow us to begin again. Pour the bleach in the water and watch it become "pure" again. Remind children that we need to continue to confess our sins to God.

"Now that you have purified yourselves by obeying the truth so that you have sincere love for your brothers, love one another deeply, from the heart."

—*1 Peter 1:22*